1000 PERSIAN SENTENCES:
Dual Language Persian-English Interlinear & Parallel Text

PERSIAN BOOKS AND AUDIO BY L2 PRESS

PERSIAN GRAMMAR BY EXAMPLE: Dual Language Persian-English, Interlinear & Parallel Text

1000 PERSIAN SENTENCES: Dual Language Persian-English, Interlinear & Parallel Text

These two books provide over 1500 sentences of interlinear + parallel text plus audio for maximum comprehension of every word and sentence.

1000 PERSIAN SENTENCES:
Dual Language Persian-English Interlinear & Parallel Text

Copyright © 2021 by Aron Levin

All Rights Reserved. No part of this book, or associated audio files, may be reproduced, stored in a retrieval system, or transmitted, in any form or by any means, electronic, mechanical, photocopying, recording, internet usage, or otherwise, without the prior written permission from the publisher.

ISBN 978-1-952161-06-3

www.L2Press.com

First Edition

Table of contents

Introduction — i

Alphabet and Pronunciation — iv

1000 Sentences — 1

Introduction

Dear Language Learner: This book is intended for beginner and intermediate learners of Modern Persian who want to improve their Persian vocabulary, grammar, speaking, and listening abilities through massive exposure to one thousand wide-ranging sentences.

The sentences are presented in an *interlinear + parallel text* format for maximum comprehension of every aspect of the sentence. On the right side of the page is the interlinear Persian, romanization, and translation. Linguistically speaking, this is an interlinear gloss containing three lines of interlinear text: (1) the first line is the Persian source text; (2) the second line is the romanization, which improves speaking ability and provides a better overall understanding of the word; and (3) the third line is the translation, which gives more context-specific information than a dictionary possibly could. On the left side of the page is the parallel text, which is an English translation of the Persian sentence. The translation style of the parallel text is a free translation, whereas the third line of the interlinear gloss is essentially a literal translation.

A Persian audio file recorded by a professional voice actor is available as a companion to this book (available for purchase at L2Press.com). Audio files are important for developing correct pronunciation and listening ability. The second line of the interlinear is an excellent pronunciation guide, but there is no replacement for trying to emulate the pronunciation of a native speaker when it comes to developing a good accent.

How To Use This Book

Mastering the meaning, pronunciation, and usage of every sentence in this book will tremendously improve your Persian reading and speaking proficiency. Once you deeply understand this wide swath of Persian vocabulary and sentence structures, all future Persian-learning endeavors will be much more fruitful, reading native Persian materials will be far easier, and your speaking and listening abilities will be greatly enhanced. How does one master all of the material in this book? Here are tips to get you started:

1. *Extensive and Intensive reading.* Intensive reading is a way of reading a small amount of text in a detailed manner with the goal of understanding as much as possible while extracting new vocabulary and grammar. Extensive reading is reading quickly, for pleasure, without looking up anything, for as long as you want, with the goal of gaining massive exposure to the language.

   This book allows language learners at any stage to easily perform both intensive and extensive reading. If you want to improve your speaking abilities, then read aloud. If you aren't sure of the correct pronunciation, then look at the line below for immediate feedback and correction. And if you don't know the meaning of the word, look at the third line for immediate feedback and correction of the meaning. If you don't understand the meaning of a phrase or sentence, then look at the parallel text. This constant cycle of instant feedback and correction is a key attribute of deliberate practice and will accelerate your learning like never before.

2. *Active listening.* Written text with a corresponding audio file is a powerful combination of language learning tools. By hearing the language spoken, you can appreciate and imitate the prosody, melody, and intonation of the language. Combined, the audio and romanization will instill confidence, consistency, and clarity in how the language is spoken.

Introduction

Prioritize active listening, which requires all of your attention and concentration, over passive listening, which requires little effort and yields minimal results. Productive active listening exercises include:

- *Shadowing*: listen to audio while repeating it nearly simultaneously, directly following the sound like a shadow. Ideally do this both with and without looking at a written version of the audio. Try to speak, as best as you can, like the native speaker, focusing on vowel sounds, vowel length, new consonant sounds, stress, and intonation.
- *Repeating*: listen to audio and then pause to repeat. Like shadowing, ideally do this both with and without looking at a written version of the audio, and try to mimic the native speaker as closely as possible. This technique, along with shadowing, is useful for developing a good accent.
- *Listening-Reading*: listen to Persian audio while reading English text. Following along in English while listening to Persian audio helps you understand what is being said. Can also combine this technique with shadowing (Listen to Persian, shadow in Persian, read English). This technique is great for developing your ability to understand spoken Persian.
- *Transcribing*: listen to an audio file while pausing frequently to write down exactly what you heard. Correct your transcription against the original text. This technique is good for *focused* listening comprehension.

3. *Spaced repetition with chunks.* Spaced repetition software (SRS) is an electronic flashcard system with a built-in algorithm that shows you the cards at optimal times for memorizing. If you are having trouble remembering certain words, phrases, and sentences after reading them many times, and you like to review flashcards, then put them into an SRS, such as Anki or Memrise, and review daily. "Chunks" are groups of two or more words that you should learn as a single unit. Chunks give you vocabulary, context, and grammar all in a short phrase. As an example, take the simple sentence "Last night I ate dinner with my family." Instead of breaking up the sentence into eight individual words and learning them all separately, it would be far more productive to learn it in three chunks - "last night", "I ate dinner", and "with my family". Now you know three chunks of words that work together and can be applied in new situations. "I was at my friend's house *last night*", "*I ate dinner* already", "I'm visiting New York *with my family*". Intuiting the grammar through context is more enjoyable and useful than laboring through tedious grammar exercises.

4. *Converse with a speaking partner.* In parallel to mastering the content of this book using the above techniques, find a native speaker and converse with them on a consistent basis, preferably at least one hour per week. The ideal practice partner is patient and will not simply correct your errors but will prompt you to self-correct. If you desire to speak fluently, there is no substitute for conversation practice.

Special notes about the Persian

1. The direct object particle را - *raa* does not have an English translation and is therefore labeled "D.O.", for "direct object", in the third line of the interlinear. It is used only before *definite* direct objects and not before *indefinite* direct objects. See the *Persian Grammar By Example* book for a more comprehensive description with examples.

2. The interrogative particle آیا - *aayaa* does not have an English translation and is therefore labeled "I.P.", for "interrogative particle", in the third line of the interlinear. It appears at the beginning of a sentence,

and its function is to indicate that a question is being asked. It is used primarily in written Persian and rarely in spoken Persian.

3. *He* vs. *she* vs *s/he* vs. *it*: Since Persian verbs are not conjugated by grammatical gender, a pronoun is provided next to the verb purely based on the context of the sentence. "It" is used when referring to a non-human object, "he" or "she" is used when the gender of the person is clear (e.g., mom, dad, etc), and "s/he" is used when the gender of the person is unclear.

Alphabet and Pronunciation

		The Persian Alphabet and Transliteration				
Letter name	IPA	Transliteration	End	Middle	Beginning	Isolated
alef	*takes vowel sound*	*takes vowel sound*	ـا	ـا	آ/ا	ا
be	/b/	b	ـب	ـبـ	بـ	ب
pe	/p/	p	ـپ	ـپـ	پـ	پ
te	/t/	t	ـت	ـتـ	تـ	ت
se	/s/	s	ـث	ـثـ	ثـ	ث
jim	/dʒ/	j	ـج	ـجـ	جـ	ج
che	/tʃ/	ch	ـچ	ـچـ	چـ	چ
he	/h/	h	ـح	ـحـ	حـ	ح
khe	/x/	kh	ـخ	ـخـ	خـ	خ
daal	/d/	d	ـد	ـد	د	د
zaal	/z/	z	ـذ	ـذ	ذ	ذ
re	/ɾ/	r	ـر	ـر	ر	ر
ze	/z/	z	ـز	ـز	ز	ز
zhe	/ʒ/	zh	ـژ	ـژ	ژ	ژ
sin	/s/	s	ـس	ـسـ	سـ	س
shin	/ʃ/	sh	ـش	ـشـ	شـ	ش
saad	/s/	s	ـص	ـصـ	صـ	ص
zaad	/z/	z	ـض	ـضـ	ضـ	ض
taa	/t/	t	ـط	ـطـ	ط	ط
zaa	/z/	z	ـظ	ـظـ	ظ	ظ
eyn	/ʔ/	'	ـع	ـعـ	عـ	ع
qeyn	/ɣ/	q	ـغ	ـغـ	غـ	غ
fe	/f/	f	ـف	ـفـ	فـ	ف
qaaf	/ɣ/	q	ـق	ـقـ	قـ	ق
kaaf	/k/	k	ـک	ـکـ	کـ	ک
gaaf	/g/	g	ـگ	ـگـ	گـ	گ
laam	/l/	l	ـل	ـلـ	لـ	ل
mim	/m/	m	ـم	ـمـ	مـ	م
nun	/n/	n	ـن	ـنـ	نـ	ن
vaav	/v/, /uː/, /o/	v, u, o	ـو	ـو	و	و
he	/h/	h	ـه	ـهـ	هـ	ه
ye	/j/	y	ـی	ـیـ	یـ	ی

Persian Vowels

Transliteration[A]	IPA[B]	Similar to this English sound[C]
a	/æ/	b<u>a</u>t
aa	/ɒː/	p<u>a</u>lm
e	/e/	p<u>e</u>t
o	/o/	gl<u>o</u>ry
i	/iː/	gl<u>ee</u>
u	/uː/	fl<u>u</u>te
ey	/ej/	th<u>ey</u>
ow	/ow/	gl<u>ow</u>

(A) The first column lists vowels used in the transliteration of Persian in this book.
(B) The middle column shows the phonemic notation for each transliterated vowel.
(C) The third and final column lists English words with comparable vowel sounds. The relevant vowel is underlined. Keep in mind that these are just approximations.

1000 Sentences

(1) A big wedding with many people is our tradition.

ما رسم داریم عروسی بزرگ، با تعداد زیادی مهمان بگیریم.
maa rasm daarim 'arusi_ye bozorg baa te'daad_e ziyaadi mehmaan begirim
we tradition we have wedding big with number many guest we would get

(2) A bottle of mineral water and two glasses please.

یک بطری آب معدنی و دو لیوان لطفاً.
yek botri aab ma'dani va do livaan lotfan
a bottle water mineral and two glass please

(3) A family with three children lives next door.

خانواده‌ای با سه فرزند، در خانه‌ی کناری، زندگی می‌کنند.
khaanevaadeiy baa se farzand dar khaane_ye kenaari zendegi mikonand
a family with three child at house next they live

(4) One of our friends is a chef at a fancy restaurant.

یکی از دوستان ما، در یک رستوران مجلل سرآشپز است.
yeki az dustaan_e maa dar yek resturaan_e mojallal saraashpaz ast
one of our friends at a restaurant fancy chef s/he is

(5) A healthy diet is important if you want to live a long time.

اگر عمر طولانی می‌خواهید، رژیم غذایی مناسب مهم است.
agar omr_e tulaani mikhaahid rezhim_e qazaaei_ye monaaseb mohemm ast
if life long you want diet suitable important it is

(6) A horse walks into a bar, and the bartender asks, "Why the long face?".

اسبی وارد یک بار می‌شود و متصدی بار از او می‌پرسد: «چرا اینقدر دمغی؟»
asbi vaared_e yek baar mishavad va motesaddi_ye baar az u miporsad cheraa inqadr damaqi
a horse s/he enters a bar and it becomes bartender bar from s/he s/he asks why so you're sad

1

(7) A little exercise is healthy, but you should not overdo it.

کمی ورزش باعث تندرستی است، اما نباید در انجام آن افراط کنید.

kami varzesh baaes_e tandorosti ast, ammaa nabaayad dar anjaam_e aan efraat konid.
a little exercise cause healthy it is but should not at doing that you should overdo

(8) A mechanic is fixing my car.

یک مکانیک دارد ماشینم را تعمیر می‌کند.

yek mekaanik daarad maashinam raa ta'miyr mikonad.
a mechanic ←s/he is my car D.O. repair s/he does→

(9) A new shopping center is being built here.

دارند مرکز خرید جدیدی در اینجا می‌سازند.

daarand markaz_e kharid_e jadidi dar injaa misaazand.
←they are center shopping new at here they build→

(10) A picture of my children is hanging above my desk.

تصویری از فرزندانم، بالای میزم آویزان است.

tasviri az farzandaanam, baalaa_ye mizam aavizaan ast.
a picture from my children above my desk hanging it is

(11) A recent study shows that pollution is still increasing.

یک مطالعه‌ی جدید نشان می‌دهد که آلودگی همچنان در حال افزایش است.

yek motaale'e_ye jadid neshaan midahad ke aaludegi hamchenaan dar haal_e afzaayesh ast.
a study new it shows that pollution still increasing it is

(12) A small band played at our wedding.

گروه موسیقی کوچکی، در مراسم عروسی ما نواختند.

goruh_e musiqi_ye kuchaki, dar maraasem_e 'arusi_ye maa navaakhtand.
group music a small at ceremony our wedding they played

(13) According to the weather forecast, it will rain tomorrow.

طبق پیش‌بینی آب و هوا، فردا باران خواهد بارید.

tebq_e pishbini_ye aab o havaa, fardaa baaraan khaahad baarid.
according to forecast weather tomorrow rain it will pour

(14) Addiction to opioids is a big problem.

اعتیاد به مواد مخدر مشکل بزرگی است.

e'tiyaad be mavaadd_e mokhadder moshkel_e bozorgi ast.
addiction to opioids problem a big it is

(15) Adults must pay, but admission is free for kids.

بزرگسالان باید پرداخت کنند، اما پذیرش برای بچه‌ها رایگان است.

bozorgsaalaan baayad pardaakht konand, ammaa paziresh baraaye bachchehaa raayegaan ast.
adults must they must pay but admission for kids free it is

(16) After the first half, our team leads 2-0.	پس از نیمه‌ی اول، تیم ما دو-صفر جلو است. pas az nime_ye avval tim_e maa do-sefr jelo ast after half first our team two-one ahead it is
(17) After the meal there was a delicious dessert.	پس از غذا، دسر خوشمزه‌ای بود. pas az qazaa deser_e khoshmazeiy bud after meal dessert a delicious it was
(18) After we ate, we went for a walk.	پس از خوردن غذا، قدم زدیم. pas az khordan_e qazaa qadam zadim after eating food we walked
(19) Ahmed came here to study English.	احمد برای تحصیل زبان انگلیسی به اینجا آمده است. ahmad baraaye tahsil_e zabaan_e engelisi be injaa aamade ast Ahmed for study language English to here he has come
(20) All group members were present at the meeting.	همه‌ی اعضای گروه در جلسه حضور داشتند. hame_ye a'zaa_ye goruh dar jalase hozur daashtand all members group at meeting presence they had
(21) All the protests achieved nothing.	هیچ یک از اعتراضات به نتیجه نرسید. hich yek az e'teraazaat be natije naresid none of protests to outcome it didn't reach
(22) Always go to other people's funerals, otherwise they won't come to yours.	همیشه به مراسم خاک‌سپاری افراد دیگر بروید، hamishe be maraasem_e khaak sepaari_ye afraad_e digar beravid always to ceremony funeral people other go در غیر این صورت، آنها به مراسم خاک‌سپاری شما dar qeyr_e in surat aanhaa be maraasem_e khaak sepaari_ye shomaa otherwise they to ceremony your funeral نخواهند آمد. nakhaahand aamad they won't come
(23) Anything else? - No, that's all.	چیز دیگری هست؟ - نه، همش همین بود. chiz_e digari hast na hamash hamin bud thing other it is no all of it this it was
(24) Are there any leftovers from dinner?	از شام چیزی باقی مانده است؟ az shaam chizi baaqi maande ast from dinner something it has remained

(25)	با اتوبوس می‌رویم یا با مترو؟ baa otobus miravim yaa baa metro with bus we go or with subway	Are we going by bus or subway?
(26)	امشب بیرون می‌رویم؟ emshab birun miravim tonight outside we go	Are we going out tonight?
(27)	هنوز قرارست ساعت هشت و نیم همدیگر را ببینیم؟ hanuz qaraarast saa'at_e hasht o nim hamdigar raa bebinim still (it is) meeting hour eight and half each other D.O. we may see	Are we still meeting at half past eight?
(28)	تو هم می‌آیی؟ - البته! to ham miaaiy albatte you too you come of course	Are you coming? - Of course!
(29)	تو این تابستان کار خاصی انجام می‌دهی؟ نمی‌دانم، to in taabestaan kaar_e khaassi anjaam midahiy nemidaanam to in this summer activity special you do I don't know هنوز هیچ برنامه‌ای ندارم. hanuz hich barnaameiy nadaaram still none plan I don't have	Are you doing anything special this summer? - I don't know, we don't have any plans yet.
(30)	آیا شما با ممنوعیت سیگار کشیدن در مکان‌های aayaa shomaa baa mamnu'iyyat_e sigaar keshidan dar makaanhaa_ye I.P. you with prohibition cigarette smoking at places عمومی موافقید یا مخالف؟ - من با آن موافقم. 'omumi mowaafeqid yaa mokhaalef man baa aan mowaafeqam public you agree or oppose I with that I'm agreeing	Are you for or against a ban on smoking in public? - I am for it.
(31)	آیا نقدی پرداخت می‌کنید؟ می‌توانید با کارت اعتباری aayaa naqdi pardaakht mikonid mitavaanid baa kaart_e e'tebaari I.P. cash you pay you can with card debit نیز پرداخت کنید. niz pardaakht konid also you may pay	Are you paying with cash? You can also pay by debit card.
(32)	مطمئنی کتابخانه امروز باز است؟ فکر می‌کردم بسته motma'enniy ketaabkhaane emruz baaz ast fekr mikardam baste you are sure library today open it is I thought closed باشد. baashad it may be	Are you sure that the library is open today? I thought it was closed.

(33) Are you well rested? We have a busy day ahead of us.

خوب استراحت کرده‌ای؟ روز شلوغی پیش رویمان داریم.

khub well / *esteraahat* rest / *kardeiy* you have done / *ruz_e* day / *sholuqi* busy / *pish_e ruyemaan* ahead of us / *daarim* we have

(34) As soon as I know the date of the wedding, I'll let you know.

به محض اینکه تاریخ عروسی را بدانم، به شما خبر می‌دهم.

be mahz_e inke as soon as / *taarikh_e* date / *'arusi* wedding / *raa* D.O. / *bedaanam* I would know / *be* to / *shomaa* you / *khabar* notice / *midaham* I give

(35) At home we often eat spicy food.

در خانه اغلب غذای تند می‌خوریم.

dar at / *khaane* home / *aqlab* often / *qazaa_ye* food / *tond* spicy / *mikhorim* we eat

(36) At our company we make home furniture like couches and tables.

شرکت ما اسباب و اثاثیه منزل، مثل کاناپه و میز درست می‌کند.

sherkat_e maa our company / *asbaab va asaasiye_ye* furniture / *manzel* home / *mesl_e* like / *kaanaape* couch / *va* and / *miz* table / *dorost mikonad* it makes

(37) At the moment there are no tables available.

در حال حاضر، میزی موجود نیست.

dar haal_e at moment / *haazer* present / *mizi* a table / *mojud* available / *nist* it is not

(38) At the zoo they have 34 different species of birds.

در باغ وحش، آنها سی و چهار گونه‌ی مختلف پرنده دارند.

dar at / *baaq_e vahsh* zoo / *aanhaa* they / *si yo chahaar* thirty-four / *gune_ye* species / *mokhtalef_e* different / *parande* bird / *daarand* they have

(39) Be quiet. The kids are already sleeping.

ساکت باشید. بچه‌ها خواب هستند.

saaket quiet / *baashid* be / *bachchehaa* kids / *khaab* asleep / *hastand* they are

(40) Before we go to the party, I want to change into a nicer outfit.

قبل از اینکه به مهمانی برویم، می‌خواهم لباس زیباتری بپوشم.

qabl az before / *inke* that / *be* to / *mehmaani* party / *beravim* we would go / *mikhaaham* I want / *lebaas_e* dress / *zibaatari* a more beautiful / *bepusham* I would wear

(41) Biking on the sidewalk is not allowed.

دوچرخه سواری در پیاده‌رو مجاز نیست.
docharkhe savaari dar piyaadero mojaaz nist
bicycle riding at sidewalk allowed it is not

(42) Bon appétit! / Enjoy your meal!

نوش جان! / از غذای خود لذت ببرید!
nush_e jaan az qazaa_ye khod lezzat bebarid
bon appétit from food self enjoy

(43) Both of my children have brown eyes.

هر دو فرزندم چشمان قهوه‌ای دارند.
har do farzandam cheshmaan_e qahveiy daarand
every two my child eyes brown they have

(44) Both the checking and savings accounts are free.

هر دو حساب کوتاه‌مدت و بلندمدت رایگان هستند.
har do hesaab_e kutaahmoddat va bolandmoddat raayegaan hastand
both account short-term and long-term free they are

(45) Bye. See you soon!

خداحافظ. به زودی می‌بینمت!
khodaahaafez be zudi mibinamat
goodbye to soon I see you

(46) Call this number in case of emergency.

در موارد اضطراری، با این شماره تماس بگیرید.
dar mavaared_e ezteraari baa in shomaare tamaas begirid
in cases emergency with this number call

(47) Calm down, please. Everything is okay.

لطفاً آرام باشید. همه چیز خوب است.
lotfan aaraam baashid hame chiz khub ast
please calm be everything good it is

(48) Can anyone beat the world champion?

کسی می‌تواند قهرمان جهان را شکست دهد؟
kasi mitavaanad qahremaan_e jahaan raa shekast dahad
someone s/he can champion world D.O. s/he may beat

(49) Can I borrow your toothbrush? - No, that's disgusting!

می‌توانم مسواک شما را قرض بگیرم؟ - نه، این حال به هم زن است!
mitavaanam mesvaak_e shomaa raa qarz begiram na in
I can your toothbrush D.O. I may borrow no this
haal be ham zan ast
disgusting it is

(50) Can I get another blanket? I'm cold.

می‌توانم پتوی دیگری داشته باشم؟ سردم است.
mitavaanam patu_ye digari daashte baasham sardam ast
I can blanket another I may have my cold it is

(51) Can I have an appointment immediately? - Unfortunately that is not possible.

می‌توانم وقت ملاقات فوری بگیرم؟ - متأسفانه
mitavaanam vaqt_e molaaqaat_e fori begiram — moteassefaane
I can appointment immediate I may take unfortunately

امکان‌پذیر نیست.
emkaanpazir nist
possible it is not

(52) Can I pay by credit card?

می‌توانم با کارت اعتباری پرداخت کنم؟
mitavaanam baa kaart_e e'tebaari pardaakht konam
I can with card credit I may pay

(53) Can I print this on your printer?

می‌توانم این را با چاپگر شما چاپ کنم؟
mitavaanam in raa baa chaapgar_e shomaa chaap konam
I can this D.O. with your printer I may print

(54) Can I talk to you briefly?

می‌توانم مختصری با شما صحبت کنم؟
mitavaanam mokhtasari baa shomaa sohbat konam
I can briefly with you I may speak

(55) Can you call me again later? We are eating right now.

می‌توانید بعداً دوباره با من تماس بگیرید؟ الان داریم
mitavaanid ba'dan dobaare baa man tamaas begirid alaan daarim
you can later again with I you may call now we are →

غذا می‌خوریم.
qazaa mikhorim
food we eat →

(56) Can you help me? I can't lift the box alone.

می‌توانید به من کمک کنید؟ من نمی‌توانم جعبه را
mitavaanid be man komak konid man nemitavaanam ja'be raa
you can to I you may help I I can't box D.O.

به تنهایی بلند کنم.
be tanhaayi boland konam
alone I could lift

(57) Can you help your grandpa set up his new computer?

می‌توانید به پدربزرگتان کمک کنید تا کامپیوتر جدید
mitavaanid be pedarbozorgetaan komak konid taa kaampiyuter_e jadid_e
you can to your grandfather you may help so computer new

خود را راه‌اندازی کند؟
khod raa raahandaazi konad
self D.O. he would set up

(58) **Can you let me know by tomorrow morning?**
می‌توانی تا فردا صبح به من خبر بدهی؟
mitavaani taa fardaa sobh be man khabar bedahi
you can until tomorrow morning to I may inform

(59) **Can you please speak a little louder?**
می‌توانید لطفاً کمی بلندتر صحبت کنید؟
mitavaanid lotfan kami bolandtar sohbat konid
you can please a little louder you may speak

(60) **Can you please turn on the light? I can't see anything.**
می‌توانید چراغ را روشن کنید، لطفاً؟ من نمی‌توانم
mitavaanid cheraaq raa roshan konid lotfan man nemitavaanam
you could light D.O. you may turn on please I I can't

چیزی ببینم.
chizi bebinam
anything I can see

(61) **Can you take the dog to the vet today?**
می‌توانید امروز سگ را به دامپزشکی ببرید؟
mitavaanid emruz sag raa be daampezeshki bebarid
you can today dog D.O. to veterinary you may take

(62) **Can you turn down the volume, please?**
می‌توانید صدا را کم کنید، لطفاً؟
mitavaanid sedaa raa kam konid lotfan
you can volume D.O. you can turn down please

(63) **Carola spends a lot of money on her hobbies.**
کارولا پول زیادی خرج سرگرمی‌هایش می‌کند.
kaarola pul_e ziyaadi kharj_e sargarmihaayash mikonad
Carola money much ←she spends her hobbies she does→

(64) **Caution! The floor is wet.**
احتیاط! زمین خیس است.
ehtiyaat zamin khis ast
caution ground wet it is

(65) **Children are financially dependent on their parents.**
فرزندان از لحاظ مالی به والدین خود وابسته هستند.
farzandaan az lahaaz_e maali be vaaledeyn_e khod vaabaste hastand
children from aspect financial to parents self dependent they are

(66) **Children over 10 years old pay the full entrance fee.**
کودکان بالای ده سال باید ورودیه‌ی کامل بپردازند.
kudakaan_e baalaa_ye dah saal baayad vorudiye_ye kaamel bepardaazand
children over ten years must entrance complete they must pay

(67) **Class is canceled next week.**
کلاس هفته‌ی بعد لغو شده است.
kelaas_e hafte_ye ba'd laqv shode ast
class week next it has been canceled

Coffee or tea? - I would prefer tea.	(68) قهوه یا چای؟ - چای را ترجیح می‌دهم. *qahve yaa chaay — chaay raa tarjih midaham* coffee or tea — tea D.O. I prefer
Come here so that I can show you something.	(69) بیا اینجا تا چیزی را به تو نشان بدهم. *biyaa injaa taa chizi raa be to neshaan bedaham* come here so something D.O. to you I would show
Come in, the door is open.	(70) بیا تو! در باز است. *biyaa tu dar baaz ast* come inside door open it is
Come, we'll sit on that bench over there.	(71) بیا روی نیمکت آنجا بنشینیم. *biyaa ru_ye nimkat aanjaa beneshinim* come on bench there we would sit
Congratulations on the birth of your daughter.	(72) تولد دخترتان مبارک! *tavallod_e dokhtaretaan mobaarak* birth your daughter it may be blessed
Could you call again later?	(73) می‌توانید دوباره تماس بگیرید؟ *mitavaanid dobaare tamaas begirid* you can again you may call
Could you give me an example?	(74) می‌توانی برایم مثالی بزنی؟ *mitavaani baraayam mesaali bezani* you can for me an example you may give
Cut an onion into small pieces and fry it together with the meat.	(75) پیازی را به تکه‌های کوچک خرد کرده و آن را *piyaazi raa be tekkehaa_ye kuchak khord karde va aan raa* an onion D.O. to pieces small chop and that D.O. همراه با گوشت سرخ کنید. *hamraah baa gusht sorkh konid* along with meat fry
Dad, can you help me with my homework?	(76) پدر! می‌توانی به من در انجام تکالیفم کمک کنی؟ *pedar mitavaani be man dar anjaam_e takaalifam komak koni* father you can to I at doing my homework you can help
Day-to-day life is sometimes boring.	(77) زندگی روزمره گاهی کسل کننده است. *zendegi_ye ruzmarre gaahi kesel konande ast* life day-to-day sometimes boring it is

9

(78) Despite having the flu, I went to work, which was a terrible idea.

با وجود اینکه آنفولانزا داشتم سر کار رفتم، که فکر
baa vojud_e inke aanfulaanzaa daashtam sar_e kaar raftam ke fekr_e
even though flu I had to work I went that idea

خیلی بدی بود.
kheyli badi bud
very bad it was

(79) Did anyone witness the accident?

آیا کسی شاهد حادثه بود؟
aayaa kasi shaahed_e haadese bud
I.P. anyone s/he witnessed accident s/he was

(80) Did you come by foot or bike?

پیاده آمدی یا با دوچرخه؟
piyaade aamadi yaa baa docharkhe
on foot you came or with bicycle

(81) Did you enjoy your meal?

از غذا خوشتان آمد؟
az qazaa khoshetaan aamad
from food you liked

(82) Did you get here by car? - No, I walked.

با ماشین به اینجا آمدید؟ - نه، پیاده آمدم.
baa maashin be injaa aamadid na piyaade aamadam
with car to here you came no on foot I came

(83) Did you sleep well?

خوب خوابیدی؟
khub khaabidi
well you slept

(84) Did you wrap your mother's gift?

هدیه‌ی مادرت را کادوپیچ کردی؟
hediye_ye maadarat raa kaadopich kardi
gift your mother D.O. gift-wrap you did

(85) Dinner is nearly ready.

شام تقریباً آماده است.
shaam taqriban aamaade ast
dinner almost ready it is

(86) Dissolve the tablet in water, don't chew it.

قرص را در آب حل کنید، آن را نجوید.
qors raa dar aab hal konid aan raa najavid
tablet D.O. in water dissolve that D.O. don't chew

(87) Do monkeys actually like to eat bananas, or is that just a myth?

آیا میمون‌ها واقعاً دوست دارند موز بخورند، یا
aayaa meymunhaa vaaqe'an dust daarand moz bokhorand yaa
I.P. monkeys really they like banana they would eat or

این فقط یک افسانه است؟
in faqat yek afsaane ast
this only a myth it is

(88) Do not believe everything you are told. It is often a lie.

هر چیزی را که به شما می‌گویند باور نکنید. معمولاً
har chizi raa ke be shomaa miguyand baavar nakonid. ma'mulan
every thing D.O. that to you they tell don't believe usually

دروغ است.
doruq ast
lie it is

(89) Do not cross the street while the light is red. That is dangerous.

زمانی که چراغ قرمز است از خیابان عبور نکنید. این
zamaani ke cheraaq qermez ast az khiyaabaan 'obur nakonid. in
when that light red it is from street don't cross this

کار خطرناکی است.
kaar_e khatarnaaki ast
activity dangerous it is

(90) Do vegetarians eat eggs?

آیا گیاه‌خواران تخم مرغ می‌خورند؟
aayaa giyaahkhaaraan tokhm_e morq mikhorand
I.P. vegetarians egg they eat

(91) Do you believe in God?

آیا به خدا اعتقاد داری؟
aayaa be khodaa e'teqaad daari
I.P. in God belief you have

(92) Do you have a cream for dry skin?

کرم برای پوست خشک دارید؟
kerem baraaye pust_e khoshk daarid
cream for skin dry you have

(93) Do you have a driver's license yet?

آیا اصلاً گواهینامه‌ی رانندگی دارید؟
aayaa aslan govaahinaame_ye raanandegi daarid
I.P. at all license driving you have

(94) Do you have a ladder I can borrow? I want to clean the windows.

شما یک نردبان دارید که من بتوانم آن را
shomaa yek nardebaan daarid ke man betavaanam aan raa
you a ladder you have that I I could that D.O.

قرض بگیرم؟ می‌خواهم پنجره‌ها را تمیز کنم.
qarz begiram? mikhaaham panjerehaa raa tamiz konam
I can borrow I want windows D.O. I would clean

(95) Do you have a vase for the flowers?

برای گل‌ها، گلدان دارید؟
baraaye golhaa goldaan daarid
for flowers vase you have

(96) Do you have all the ingredients necessary to make dinner?

همه‌ی مواد لازم برای شام درست کردن را دارید؟
hame_ye mavaadd_e laazem baraaye shaam dorost kardan raa daarid
all materials necessary for dinner making D.O. you have

(97) Do you have an umbrella with you in case it rains?

اگر باران بیاید، چتر با خود دارید؟
agar baaraan biyaayad, chatr baa khod daarid
if rain it may come umbrella with self you have

(98) Do you have any book recommendations?

آیا کتابی را پیشنهاد می‌کنید؟
aayaa ketaabi raa pishnehaad mikonid
I.P. a book D.O. you recommend

(99) Do you have coins for the machine? I only have bills.

شما برای دستگاه سکه دارید؟ من فقط اسکناس دارم.
shomaa baraaye dastgaah sekke daarid man faqat eskenaas daaram
you for machine coin you have I only bill I have

(100) Do you have headaches frequently? If so, then you should not sit at the computer for so long.

آیا گاه و بیگاه سردرد دارید؟ در این صورت، نباید
aayaa gaah o bigaah sardard daarid dar in surat, nabaayad
I.P. often headache you have in this case must not

مدت طولانی پای کامپیوتر بنشینید.
moddat_e tulaani paa_ye kaampiyuter beneshinid
time long at computer you may sit

(101) Do you have medicine for a cough?

دارویی برای سرفه دارید؟
daaruiy baraaye sorfe daarid
a drug for cough you have

(102) Do you have my new address?

آدرس جدید من را دارید؟
aadres_e jadid_e man raa daarid
address my new D.O. you have

(103) Do you hear the thunder? The storm is getting closer.

صدای رعد و برق را می‌شنوید؟ طوفان دارد
sedaa_ye ra'd o barq raa mishenavid tufaan daarad
sound thunder and lightning D.O you hear storm it is →

نزدیک‌تر می‌شود.
nazdiktar mishavad
closer it becomes →

(104) Do you know a good recipe for vegetable soup?

آیا دستور تهیه‌ی خوبی برای سوپ سبزیجات بلدید؟
aayaa dastur_e tahiyye_ye khubi baraaye sup_e sabzijaat baladid
I.P. recipe good for soup vegetable you know

(105) Do you know how to swim?

آیا شنا کردن بلدید؟
aayaa shenaa kardan baladid
I.P. swimming you know

(106) Do you know the difference between vertical and horizontal?

آیا تفاوت میان عمودی و افقی را می‌دانید؟
aayaa tafaavot miyaan_e 'amudi va ofoqi raa midaanid
I.P. difference between vertical and horizontal D.O. you know

(107) Do you mind if I stop by tomorrow afternoon?

اشکالی ندارد فردا بعد از ظهر به شما سر بزنم؟
eshkaali nadaarad fardaa ba'd az zohr be shomaa sar bezanam
a problem it doesn't have tomorrow after noon to you I may stop by

(108) Do you own your house or do you rent?

شما صاحبخانه هستید یا مستأجر؟
shomaa saahebkhaane hastid yaa mostajer
you landlord you are or tenant

(109) Do you play a musical instrument?

بلدید یک ساز موسیقی بنوازید؟
baladid yek saaz_e musiqi benavaazid
you know a instrument musical you can play

(110) Do you promise not to tell anyone?

آیا قول می‌دهید به کسی نگویید؟
aayaa qol midahid be kasi naguiyd
I.P. you promise to somebody you may not tell

(111) Do you smoke? - No, never. I don't drink alcohol either.

سیگار می‌کشید؟ - نه، هرگز! من حتی الکل هم
sigaar mikeshid na hargez man hattaa alkol ham
cigarette you smoke no never I even alcohol even

نمی‌خورم.
nemikhoram
I don't drink

(112) Do you speak English? - A little.

آیا انگلیسی صحبت می‌کنید؟ - کمی.
aayaa engelisi sohbat mikonid kami
I.P. English you speak a little

(113) Do you take sugar in your tea?

چای خود را با شکر می‌خورید؟
chaay_e khod raa baa shekar mikhorid
tea self D.O. with sugar you drink

(114) Do you think that you will get the job? - Yes, I am quite optimistic.

فکر می‌کنی کار را بگیری؟ - بله، من کاملاً
fekr mikoni kaar raa begiri bale man kaamelan
you think job D.O. you may get yes I completely

خوش‌بین هستم.
khoshbin hastam
optimistic I am

(115) Do you want a receipt?

آیا رسید می‌خواهید؟
aayaa resid mikhaahid
I.P. receipt you want

(116) Do you want a ride home?

می‌خواهی به خانه برسانمت؟
mikhaahi be khaane beresaanamat
you want to home I would deliver you

(117) Does it bother you if I smoke?

اگر سیگار بکشم، اذیت می‌شوید؟
agar sigaar bekesham aziyyat mishavid
if cigarette I may smoke you are annoyed

(118) Does your family have a pet? - Yes, we have a dog.

خانواده‌ی شما حیوان خانگی دارد؟ - بله، ما یک
khaanevaade_ye shomaa heyvaan_e khaanegi daarad bale maa yek
your family pet it has yes we a

سگ داریم.
sag daarim
dog we have

(119) Doesn't everyone know that smoking is harmful to your health?

آیا همه نمی‌دانند که سیگار کشیدن برای سلامتی
aayaa hame nemidaanand ke sigaar keshidan baraaye salaamati
I.P. everyone they don't know that cigarette smoking for health

مضر است؟
mozerr ast
harmful it is

(120) Don't go into the living room with wet shoes.

با کفش خیس وارد اتاق نشیمن نشوید.
baa kafsh_e khis vaared_e otaaq_e neshiman nashavid
with shoe wet ←enter room living don't become→

(121) Don't tell me how the movie ends.

آخر فیلم را به من نگو!
aakhar_e film raa be man nagu
end movie D.O. to I don't tell

(122) Don't you have a sharper knife?

چاقوی تیزتری نداری؟
nadaari tiztari chaaqu_ye
you do not have / sharper / knife

(123) Don't you want to take off your coat?

نمی‌خواهید کتتان را در بیاورید؟
dar biyaavarid raa kotetaan nemikhaahid
you may take off / D.O. / your coat / you do not want

(124) Drive carefully. The roads are icy.

با احتیاط رانندگی کنید. جاده‌ها یخزده هستند.
hastand yakhzade jaaddehaa raanandegi konid ehtiyaat baa
they are / frozen / roads / drive / caution / with

(125) Driving eight hours is too much. You should fly instead.

هشت ساعت رانندگی، خیلی زیاد است. بهتر است با
baa ast behtar ast ziyaad kheyli raanandegi saa'at hasht
with / it is / better / it is / much / very / driving / hour / eight

هواپیما بروید.
beravid havaapeymaa
you should go / airplane

(126) Due to fog, our plane could not land.

به دلیل مه، هواپیمای ما نتوانست فرود بیاید.
biyaayad forud natavaanest havaapeymaa_ye maa meh be dalil_e
it could come / descent / it couldn't / our airplane / fog / due to

(127) Each country has its own unique culture.

هر کشوری فرهنگ منحصر به فرد خود را دارد.
daarad raa khod monhaser be fard_e farhang_e keshvari har
it has / D.O. / self / unique / culture / country / every

(128) Eight divided by two equals four.

هشت تقسیم بر دو می‌شود چهار.
chahaar mishavad do bar taqsim hasht
four / it becomes / two / by / divided / eight

(129) EU citizens can work anywhere in Europe.

شهروندان اروپایی می‌توانند هر جای اروپا کار کنند.
kaar konand orupaa jaa_ye har mitavaanand orupaaiy shahrvandaan_e
they can work / Europe / place / every / they can / European / citizens

(130) Everybody wants something different. We have to find a compromise.

هر کسی چیز متفاوتی می‌خواهد. ما باید به یک
yek be baayad maa mikhaahad motefaaveti chiz_e har kasi
a / to / must / we / s/he wants / different / thing / everybody

توافق برسیم.
beresim tavaafoq
we should arrive / compromise

(131) Everyone is talking about climate change these days.

این روزها همه درباره‌ی تغییر اقلیم صحبت می‌کنند.
sohbat mikonand eqlim taqyir_e darbaare_ye hame ruzhaa in
they talk / climate / change / about / all / days / this

(132) Everyone stood on the platform and waved goodbye.

همه روی سکو ایستادند و با دست تکان دادن خداحافظی کردند.

hame ru_ye sakku istaadand va baa dast takaan daadan khodaahaafezi kardand
all on platform they stood and with hand waving goodbye they did

(133) Everything together costs 2000 dollars including flights and hotels.

همه چیز روی هم دو هزار دلار خواهد شد که شامل پرواز و هتل هم می‌شود.

hame chiz ru_ye ham do hezaar dolaar khaahad shod ke shaamel_e parvaaz va hotel ham mishavad
everything together two thousand dollar it will be that ←it includes flight and hotel too it becomes→

(134) Excuse me for disturbing you, but there is a problem.

ببخشید که مزاحمتان می‌شوم، اما مشکلی پیش آمده است.

bebakhshid ke mozaahemetaan mishavam ammaa moshkeli pish aamade ast
excuse me that I disturb you but a problem it has happened

(135) Family is the most important thing.

خانواده مهم‌ترین چیز است.

khaanevaade mohemtarin chiz ast
family most important thing it is

(136) Feeding the animals at the zoo is forbidden.

غذا دادن به حیوانات در باغ وحش ممنوع است.

qazaa daadan be heyvaanaat dar baaq_e vahsh mamnu' ast
food giving to animals at zoo forbidden it is

(137) Finish your homework before watching television.

قبل از تماشای تلویزیون، تکلیف درسی خود را تمام کن.

qabl az tamaashaa_ye televiziyun taklif_e darsi_ye khod raa tamaam kon
before watching television homework self D.O. finish

(138) First highlight the lines, then copy and paste into a new document.

اول خطوط را هایلایت کنید، سپس آن را کپی کرده و داخل یک سند جدید بچسبانید.

avval khotut raa haaylaayt konid sepas aan raa kopi karde va daakhel_e yek sanad_e jadid bechasbaanid
first lines D.O. highlight then that D.O. copy do and inside a document new paste

(139) First put on your seat belt and then start driving.

اول کمربند خود را ببندید و سپس شروع به رانندگی کنید.

avval kamarband_e khod raa bebandid va sepas shoru' be raanandegi konid
first belt self D.O. fasten and then to begin drive do

(140) First put on your socks and then put on your shoes.

اول جوراب‌هایتان را بپوشید، بعد کفش‌ها را.

avval juraabhaayetaan raa bepushid, ba'd kafshhaa raa.
first your socks D.O. wear then shoes D.O.

(141) First we're going food shopping, then we're barbecuing in the yard.

اول مواد غذایی را می‌خریم، بعد در حیاط کباب درست می‌کنیم.

avval mavaadd_e qazaaiy raa mikharim, ba'd dar hayaat kabaab dorost mikonim.
first materials food D.O. we buy then at yard kebab we make

(142) For "marital status" you have to mark "single" since you're not married.

در قسمت «وضعیت تأهل» باید «مجرد» را علامت بزنید، چون متأهل نیستید.

dar qesmat_e vazi'yyat_e ta'ahhol baayad mojarrad raa 'alaamat bezanid, chon mote'ahhel nistid.
at section status marital must single D.O. mark because married you are not

(143) For dessert there is chocolate ice cream.

دسر بستنی شکلاتی داریم.

deser bastani_ye shokolaati daarim.
dessert ice cream chocolate we have

(144) For lunch there is chicken with rice.

ناهار مرغ با برنج داریم.

naahaar morq baa berenj daarim.
lunch chicken with rice we have

(145) For me, not only is the price important, but also the quality.

برای من، نه تنها قیمت، بلکه کیفیت نیز مهم است.

baraaye man na tanhaa qeymat balke keyfiyyat niz mohemm ast.
for I not only price but quality also important it is

(146) For the assignment you can choose from these three topics.

برای این تکلیف می‌توانید از بین این سه موضوع، انتخاب کنید.

baraaye in taklif mitavaanid az beyn_e in se mozu' entekhaab konid.
for this assignment you can from between this three topic you can choose

		(147)
For the last time, the answer is no.	برای آخرین بار، پاسخ نه است.	
	ast na paasokh baar aakharin baraaye it is no answer time last for	

		(148)
From now on I will go to the gym regularly.	از الان به بعد به صورت منظم به باشگاه می‌روم.	
	miravam baashgaah be monazzam surat_e be ba'd be alaan az I go gym to regular form to later to now from	

		(149)
Garbage collection comes twice a week.	ماشین جمع‌آوری زباله، دوبار در هفته می‌آید.	
	miaayad hafte dar dobaar zobaale jamaavari_ye maashin_e it comes week in twice garbage collection vehicle	

		(150)
Gasoline prices are much higher than normal lately.	بنزین اخیراً بسیار گران‌تر از حد معمول است.	
	ast ma'mul hadd_e az geraantar besyaar akhiran benzin it is normal limit from more expensive much lately gasoline	

		(151)
Give me a minute to think about it.	به من یک دقیقه فرصت دهید تا در مورد آن	
	aan dar mored_e taa dahid forsat daqiqe yek man be that about so give opportunity minute a I to	
	فکر کنم.	
	fekr konam I would think	

		(152)
Give me all the details about your date.	تمام جزییات مربوط به قرار عاشقانه‌ی خود را به	
	be raa khod aasheqaane_ye qaraar_e be marbut joziyyaat_e tamaam_e to D.O. self romantic date to related details all	
	من بدهید.	
	bedahid man give I	

		(153)
Green pants and yellow shoes? That looks funny.	شلوار سبز با کفش زرد؟ مسخره است.	
	ast maskhare zard kafsh_e baa sabz shalvaar_e it is ridiculous yellow shoe with green pants	

		(154)
Happy birthday!	تولدت مبارک!	
	mobaarak tavallodet it may be happy your birth	

		(155)
Have a nice weekend. - Thanks, you too.	آخر هفته‌ی خوبی داشته باشید. - ممنون، شما هم	
	ham shomaa mamnun daashte baashid khubi aakhar_e hafte_ye also you thanks you may have good weekend	
	همینطور.	
	hamintor too	

(156)	دندان‌های خود را مسواک زده‌اید؟ *mesvaak zadeiyd raa khod dandaanhaa_ye* you have brushed D.O. self teeth	Have you already brushed your teeth?
(157)	تکلیف مدرسه‌ات را انجام داده‌ای؟ *anjaam daadeiy raa madreseat taklif_e* you have done D.O. your school homework	Have you already done your homework for school?
(158)	آیا غذا خورده‌اید؟ *khordeh'id qazaa aayaa* you have eaten food I.P.	Have you already eaten?
(159)	آیا تصمیم گرفته‌اید که چه چیزی می‌خواهید *mikhaahid chizi che ke tasmim gerefteiyd aayaa* you want thing what that you have decided I.P. سفارش دهید؟ *sefaaresh dahid* you would order	Have you decided what you would like to order?
(160)	آیا تا به حال به دریای بالتیک رفته‌ای؟ *rafteiy baaltik daryaa_ye be taa be haal aayaa* you have gone Baltic sea to until now I.P.	Have you ever been to the Baltic Sea?
(161)	آیا تصادفاً عینک من را دیده‌اید؟ *dideiyd raa eynak_e man tasaadofan aayaa* you have seen D.O. my glasses accidentally I.P.	Have you, by any chance, seen my glasses?
(162)	او تکالیف من را کپی کرد، اما نمی‌دانم چطور *chetowr nemidaanam ammaa kard kopi raa takaalif_e man u* how I don't know but he did copy D.O. my homework he نمره‌ای بهتر از من گرفت. *gereft man az behtar nomreiy* he got I than better a grade	He copied my homework but somehow got a better grade than me.
(163)	او کادوهای زیادی برای تولدش گرفت. *gereft tavallodash baraaye ziyaadi kaadohaa_ye u* he got his birth for many gifts he	He got many gifts for his birthday.
(164)	او سرما خورده است و نمی‌تواند از طریق بینی *bini tariq_e az nemitavaanad va sarmaa khorde ast u* nose through from he can't and he has caught cold he نفس بکشد. *nafas bekeshad* he can breathe	He has a cold and can not breathe through his nose.

(165) He has been blind from birth.

او نابینا به دنیا آمده است.
u naabinaa be donyaa aamade ast
he blind he has been born

(166) He has been in a coma for three weeks.

او سه هفته در کما بوده است.
u se hafte dar komaa bude ast
he three week in coma he has been

(167) He hurt himself and had to go to the emergency room.

او به خودش آسیب زد و مجبور شد به اتاق اورژانس برود.
u be khodash aasib zad va majbur shod be otaaq_e urzhaans beravad
he to himself he hurt and forced he became to room emergency he would go

(168) He is an actor and also a great singer.

او بازیگر و هم چنین یک خواننده عالی است.
u baazigar va hamchenin yek khaanande_ye 'aali ast
he actor and also a singer great he is

(169) He is an average student but an excellent athlete.

او یک دانش‌آموز معمولی، اما یک ورزشکار عالی است.
u yek daaneshaamuz_e ma'muli ammaa yek varzeshkaar_e 'aali ast
he a student average but a athlete excellent he is

(170) He looks just like his father.

او دقیقاً شبیه پدرش است.
u daqiqan shabih_e pedarash ast
he exactly like his father he is

(171) He plays tennis quite well for a beginner.

او به نسبت یک مبتدی، خیلی خوب تنیس بازی می‌کند.
u be nesbat_e yek mobtadi kheyli khub tenis baazi mikonad
he in relation a beginner very well tennis he plays

(172) He ran a marathon and finished in first place.

او در ماراتن دوید و اول شد.
u dar maaraaton david va avval shod
he at marathon he ran and first he became

(173) He really deserves a vacation.

واقعاً تعطیلات حقش است.
vaaqe'an ta'tilaat haqqash ast
really vacation his right it is

(174) He refused my offer of help.

او پیشنهاد کمک من را رد کرد.
u pishnehaad_e komak_e man raa rad kard
he offer my help D.O. he refused

(175) او بیماری خیلی سختی دارد.
u bimaari_ye kheyli sakhti daarad
he illness very severe he has

He suffers from a serious illness.

(176) او فکر می‌کند باهوش‌تر از چیزیست که واقعاً هست.
u fekr mikonad baahushtar az chizist ke vaaqe'an hast
he he thinks smarter than it is something that really he is

He thinks he is smarter than he really is.

(177) او به من گفت که به مهمانی می‌آید ولی دیرتر.
u be man goft ke be mehmaani miaayad vali dirtar
he to I he said that to party he comes but later

He told me that he is coming to the party but will be late.

(178) او خیلی تلاش کرد تا چیزی خوشمزه بپزد.
u kheyli talaash kard taa chizi khoshmaze bepazad
he very he tried so something tasty he would cook

He tried very hard to cook something tasty.

(179) او فقط در صورتی شغل را قبول می‌کند که شرکت
u faqat dar surati shoql raa qabul mikonad ke sherkat
he only in case job D.O. he accepts that company

هزینه‌های جابجایی او را بپردازد.
hazinehaa_ye jaabejaai_ye u raa bepardaazad
expenses his relocation D.O. it would pay

He will only accept the job if the company pays for his moving expenses.

(180) او در تحقیقات پزشکی کار می‌کند.
u dar tahqiqaat_e pezeshki kaar mikonad
he at research medical he works

He works in medical research.

(181) او تحت فشار به خوبی کار می‌کند.
u taht_e feshaar be khubi kaar mikonad
he under pressure well he works

He works well under pressure.

(182) سلام، چطوری؟ - خوب! ممنون! شما چطور؟
salaam chetowri khub mamnun shomaa chetowr
hello how are you good thanks you how

Hello, how are you? - Good, thanks, and you?

(183) این کلیدهای آپارتمان من است. می‌توانی وقتی نیستم،
in kelidhaa_ye aapaartemaan_e man ast mitavaani vaqti nistam
this keys my apartment it is you can when I am not

به گل‌هایم آب بدهی؟
be golhaayam aab bedahi
to my flowers water you can give

Here are the keys to my apartment. Can you water my flowers while I'm gone?

(184) Here is my office number and also my cell phone number.

این شماره‌ی دفتر و نیز شماره‌ی تلفن همراه من است.
in shomaare_ye daftar va niz shomaare_ye telefon_e hamraah_e man ast.
this number office and also number my cell phone it is

(185) Here is the book I was telling you about.

این کتابی است که تعریفش را برایت می‌کردم.
in ketaabi ast ke ta'rifash raa baraayat mikardam.
this book it is that describing it D.O. for you I was doing

(186) Here is the list of ingredients needed for the cake.

این لیست مواد لازم برای کیک است.
in list_e mavaadd_e laazem baraaye keyk ast.
this list ingredients necessary for cake it is

(187) He's acting as though we never spoke about that.

او طوری رفتار می‌کند که انگار هیچ‌وقت در مورد آن قضیه صحبت نکرده‌ایم.
u tori raftaar mikonad ke engaar hichvaqt dar mored_e aan qaziyye sohbat nakardeiym.
he manner he behaves that seems never about that issue we have not spoken

(188) His dismissal from the company came as a surprise.

اخراج شدن او از شرکت، غافلگیر کننده بود.
ekhraaj shodan_e u az sherkat, qaafelgir konande bud.
dismissal he from company surprising it was

(189) Hold my hand. We're crossing the street.

دستم را بگیر! داریم از خیابان رد می‌شویم.
dastam raa begir! daarim az khiyaabaan rad mishavim.
my hand D.O. get we are from street we are crossing

(190) Housing is becoming more and more expensive.

مسکن روز به روز گران‌تر می‌شود.
maskan ruz be ruz geraantar mishavad.
housing day to day more expensive it becomes

(191) How can I dispose of my old cell phone?

چگونه می‌توانم تلفن همراه قدیمی خودم را دور بیندازم؟
chegune mitavaanam telefon_e hamraah_e qadimi_ye khodam raa dur biyandaazam?
how I can cell phone old myself D.O. I can dispose

(192) How did you come up with this idea?

چطور این ایده به ذهنت رسید؟
chetowr in ide be zehnat resid?
how this idea to your mind it arrived

(193) How did you two meet?

شما دوتا چگونه ملاقات کردید؟
shomaa dotaa chegune molaaqaat kardid
you two how you met

(194) How do you play this game? Do you know the rules?

چطور این بازی را انجام می‌دهی؟ آیا قوانین را
chetowr in baazi raa anjaam midahiy aayaa qavaanin raa
how this game D.O. you do I.P. rules D.O.

بلدی؟
baladi
you know

(195) How do you spell that word?

چگونه آن کلمه را هجی می‌کنید؟
chegune aan kalame raa hejji mikonid
how that word D.O. you spell

(196) How far is it to your friend's house? - It is very close, only ten minutes from here.

آنجا تا خانه‌ی دوست شما چقدر فاصله دارد؟
aanjaa taa khaane_ye dust_e shomaa cheqadr faasele daarad
there until house your friend how much distance it has

خیلی نزدیک است، فقط ده دقیقه از اینجا فاصله
kheyli nazdik ast, faqat dah daqiqe az injaa faasele
very close it is only ten minute from here distance

دارد.
daarad
it has

(197) How many cigarettes do you smoke a day? Anything more than zero is too many.

روزانه چند سیگار می‌کشید؟ هر چیزی بیش از صفر،
ruzaane chand sigaar mikeshid har chizi bish az sefr
daily how many cigarette you smoke anything more than zero

خیلی زیاد است.
kheyli ziyaad ast
very much it is

(198) How many countries have you visited?

تا به حال چند کشور را دیده‌ای؟
taa be haal chand keshvar raa dideiy
until now how many country D.O. you have seen

(199) How many letters does the alphabet have in your language?

الفبای زبان شما چند حرف دارد؟
alefbaa_ye zabaan_e shomaa chand harf daarad
alphabet your language how many letter it has

(200) How much money do I owe you?

چقدر پول به شما بدهکارم؟
cheqadr pul be shomaa bedehkaaram
how much money to you I owe

How old is the boss? - I don't know, I guess around fifty.	رییس چند سالش است؟ - نمی‌دانم، حدس می‌زنم حدود پنجاه. *raiys chand saalash ast nemidaanam hads mizanam hodud_e panjaah* boss how many his year it is I don't know I guess around fifty	(201)
I already called twice, but nobody answered.	قبلاً دو بار زنگ زدم، اما کسی جواب نداد. *qablan do baar zang zadam ammaa kasi javaab nadaad* before twice I called but somebody s/he did not answer	(202)
I already know several people in this city.	از قبل چندین نفر را در این شهر می‌شناسم. *az qabl chandin nafar raa dar in shahr mishenaasam* already several people D.O. in this city I know	(203)
I always buy bread from the baker, not from the supermarket.	من همیشه نان را از نانوا می‌خرم، نه از سوپر مارکت. *man hamishe naan raa az naanvaa mikharam na az supermaarket* I always bread D.O. from baker I buy not from supermarket	(204)
I always have to read my children a story in the evening.	من همیشه مجبورم عصرها یک داستان برای فرزندانم بخوانم. *man hamishe majburam 'asrhaa yek daastaan baraaye farzandaanam bekhaanam* I always I have to evenings a story for my children I should read	(205)
I always take public transportation in the city.	همیشه از حمل و نقل عمومی در شهر استفاده می‌کنم. *hamishe az haml o naql_e 'omumi dar shahr estefaade mikonam* always from transportation public at city I use	(206)
I am always exhausted after running 10 km.	همیشه پس از ده کیلومتر دویدن خسته می‌شوم. *hamishe pas az dah kilumetr davidan khaste mishavam* always after ten kilometer running tired I become	(207)
I am always very nervous during exams.	همیشه در طی امتحانات خیلی عصبی هستم. *hamishe dar tey_ye emtehaanaat kheyli 'asabi hastam* always during exams very nervous I am	(208)
I am happy with the location of the apartment.	من از موقعیت مکانی آپارتمان راضی هستم. *man az moqe'iyyat_e makaani_ye aapaartemaan raazi hastam* I from location apartment satisfied I am	(209)

(210)	I am in a hurry. I'm late.	من عجله دارم. دیرم شده است. *man 'ajale daaram diram shode ast* I hurry I have my lateness it has become
(211)	I am interested in other countries and cultures.	من به کشورها و فرهنگ‌های دیگر علاقه دارم. *man be keshvarhaa va farhanghaa_ye digar 'alaaqe daaram* I to countries and cultures other interest I have
(212)	I am lucky that all my grandchildren live nearby.	شانس آورده‌ام که همه‌ی نوه‌هایم، نزدیک من زندگی می‌کنند. *shaans aavardeam ke hame_ye navehaayam nazdik_e man zendegi mikonand* chance I have brought that all my grandchildren nearby I they live
(213)	I am new to the building. I don't know any neighbors yet.	من تازه به این ساختمان آمده‌ام. هنوز هیچ یک از همسایه‌ها را نمی‌شناسم. *man taaze be in saakhtemaan aamadeam hanuz hich yek az hamsaayehaa raa nemishenaasam* I new to this building I have come still none of neighbors D.O. I don't know
(214)	I am not hungry right now. I don't want to eat anything.	الان گرسنه نیستم. نمی‌خواهم چیزی بخورم. *alaan gorsne nistam nemikhaaham chizi bokhoram* now hungry I am not I don't want something I would eat
(215)	I am not interested in politics.	به سیاست علاقه‌ای ندارم. *be siyaasat 'alaaqeiy nadaaram* to politics interest I don't have
(216)	I am proud of you. You did a great job.	من به تو افتخار می‌کنم. کارت خیلی خوب بود. *man be to eftekhaar mikonam kaarat kheyli khub bud* I to you proud I do your work very good it was
(217)	I am quite surprised that the apartment is so cheap. I wonder what's wrong with it.	از قیمت ارزان این آپارتمان، خیلی تعجب کردم. حیران مانده‌ام که مشکلش چیست. *az qeymat_e arzaan_e in aapaartemaan kheyli ta'ajjob kardam heyraan maandeam ke moshkelash chist* from price cheap this apartment very I was surprised confused I have stayed that its problem what it is

(218) I am the youngest in our family.

من جوان‌ترین فرد خانواده‌مان هستم.
man javaantarin fard_e khaanevaademaan hastam
I youngest person our family I am

(219) I bought a digital watch. It runs more accurately than my old wind-up watch.

من یک ساعت دیجیتال خریدم. دقیق‌تر از ساعت
man yek saa'at_e dijitaal kharidam daqiqtar az saa'at_e
I a watch digital I bought more precise than watch

کوکی قدیمیم کار می‌کند.
kuki_ye qadimiyam kaar mikonad
wind up my old it works

(220) I bought a used car, not a new one.

من یک ماشین دست دوم خریدم، نه یک ماشین نو.
man yek maashin_e dast_e dovvom kharidam na yek maashin_e no
I a car second-hand I bought not a car new

(221) I bought more oranges than I know what to do with.

آنقدر پرتقال خریده‌ام که نمی‌دانم با آنها چه
aanqadr porteqaal kharideam ke nemidaanam baa aanhaa che
that much orange I have bought that I don't know with they what

کنم.
konam
I should do

(222) I bought myself a bigger computer monitor. It's better for my eyes.

برای خودم یک مانیتور رایانه‌ی بزرگ خریدم. این
baraaye khodam yek maanitor_e raayaane_ye bozorg kharidam in
for myself a monitor computer big I bought this

مانیتور برای چشم‌های من بهتر است.
maanitor baraaye cheshmhaa_ye man behtar ast
monitor for my eyes better it is

(223) I bought myself a dark blue suit.

برای خودم یک کت و شلوار آبی تیره خریدم.
baraaye khodam yek kot o shalvaar_e aabi_ye tire kharidam
for myself a coat and pants blue dark I bought

(224) I bought these sunglasses in Europe.

من این عینک آفتابی را از اروپا خریدم.
man in eynak_e aaftaabi raa az orupaa kharidam
I this glasses sun D.O. from Europe I bought

(225) I can barely move without pain.

به سختی می‌توانم بدون درد حرکت کنم.
be sakhti mitavaanam bedun_e dard harekat konam
barely I can without pain I can move

1000 Sentences

(226) I can not decide that myself because I have to ask the boss first.

من به شخصه نمی‌توانم تصمیم بگیرم، چون اول باید
man *be shakhse* *nemitavaanam* *tasmim* *begiram* *chon* *avval* *baayad*
I personally I can't decision I can take because first must

از ریس سوال کنم.
az *raiys* *soaal konam*
from boss I should ask

(227) I can speak English, French, and Persian very well.

من انگلیسی، فرانسوی و فارسی را به خوبی
man *engelisi* *faraansavi* *va* *faarsi* *raa* *be khubi*
I English French and Persian D.O. well

صحبت می‌کنم.
sohbat mikonam
I speak

(228) I can't answer my phone right now, so please leave a message.

در حال حاضر، نمی‌توانم به تماس شما پاسخ دهم،
dar *haal_e* *haazer* *nemitavaanam* *be* *tamaas_e shomaa* *paasokh* *daham*
at state present I can't to your call answer I can give

لطفاً پیغام بگذارید.
lotfan *peyqaam* *begozaarid*
please message you may put

(229) I can't eat any more. I'm stuffed.

بیشتر از این نمی‌توانم بخورم. کاملاً سیر شده‌ام.
bishtar *az* *in* *nemitavaanam* *bokhoram* *kaamelan* *sir* *shodeam*
more than this I can't I can eat completely full I've become

(230) I can't explain how the chocolate disappeared.

نمی‌توانم توضیح بدهم که شکلات چگونه
nemitaavanam *tozih* *bedaham* *ke* *shokolaat* *chegune*
I can't explanation I may give that chocolate how

ناپدید شد.
naapadid shod
it disappeared

(231) I can't find my keys anywhere.

نمی‌توانم کلیدهایم را پیدا کنم.
nemitavaanam *kelidhaayam* *raa* *peydaa konam*
I can't my keys D.O. I can find

(232) I can't hear so well anymore.

دیگر نمی‌توانم خیلی خوب بشنوم.
digar *nemitavaanam* *kheyli* *khub* *beshnavam*
anymore I can't very well I can hear

(233) I can't help you right now. I'm in the middle of cooking dinner.
الان نمی‌توانم بهت کمک کنم. دارم شام می‌پزم.
alaan nemitavaanam behet komak konam daaram shaam mipazam
now I can't to you I can help I am ← dinner → I'm cooking

(234) I can't read your handwriting.
نمی‌توانم دست‌خطت را بخوانم.
nemitavaanam dastkhattat raa bekhaanam
I can't your handwriting D.O. I can read

(235) I can't run because of pain in one of my toes.
نمی‌توانم بدوم، چون یکی از انگشت‌های پایم درد می‌کند.
nemitavaanam bedavam, chon yeki az angoshthaa_ye paayam
I can't I can run because one of fingers my foot
dard mikonad
it hurts

(236) I can't understand anything when you all speak at the same time.
وقتی همه‌ی شما با هم حرف می‌زنید، من نمی‌توانم چیزی متوجه بشوم.
vaqti hame_ye shomaa baa ham harf mizanid, man nemitavaanam
when all you together you talk I I can't
chizi motevajjeh beshavam
something I can understand

(237) I can't wait to see you again.
بی‌صبرانه منتظر دیدنت هستم.
bisabraane montazer_e didanat hastam
impatiently waiting your seeing I am

(238) I catch a cold at least once every winter.
حداقل یک بار در زمستان سرما می‌خورم.
haddeaqal yek baar dar zemestaan sarmaa mikhoram
at least one time in winter I catch a cold

(239) I changed my opinion after getting new information.
من بعد از بدست آوردن اطلاعات جدید، نظرم را عوض کردم.
man ba'd az bedast aavardan_e ettelaa'aat_e jadid, nazaram raa
I after getting information new my opinion D.O.
avaz kardam
I changed

(240) I checked the bill. Everything is correct.
صورتحساب را بررسی کردم. همه چیز درست است.
surathesaab raa barresi kardam. hame chiz dorost ast
bill D.O. I checked everything correct it is

(241) I completely forgot about the appointment.
به کلی، وقت ملاقات را فراموش کردم.
be kolli vaqt_e molaaqaat raa faraamush kardam
to whole time appointment D.O. I forgot

(242) **I cooked a special meal for you.**
یک غذای مخصوص برایت پختم.
yek qazaa_ye makhsus baraayat pokhtam
a meal special for you I cooked

(243) **I couldn't see anything because of all the dirt on the window.**
بخاطر پنجره‌های کثیف، نتوانستم هیچ چیز را
bekhaater_e panjerehaa_ye kasif natavaanestam hich chiz raa
for windows dirty I couldn't anything D.O.
ببینم.
bebinam
I could see

(244) **I did not have to pay anything. The repair was covered by the warranty.**
من پولی پرداخت نکردم، چون وارانتی شامل تعمیر
man puli pardaakht nakardam chon waarraanti shaamel_e ta'miyr
I money I did not pay because warranty ←included repair
بود.
bud
it was→

(245) **I did not realize it was already so late. I have to go.**
من متوجه نشدم که چقدر دیر شده. باید
man motevajjeh nashodam ke cheqadr dir shode baayad
I I didn't realize that how much late it has become must
بروم.
beravam
I should go

(246) **I didn't understand your question. Please repeat it.**
من سوال شما را متوجه نشدم. لطفاً تکرار کنید.
man soaal_e shomaa raa motevajjeh nashodam lotfan tekraar konid
I your question D.O. I didn't understand please repeat

(247) **I do not know if we have this shoe in your size. I'll check the stock room.**
نمی‌دانم که از این کفش اندازه پای شما داریم
nemidaanam ke az in kafsh andaaze_ye paa_ye shomaa daarim
I don't know whether of this shoe size your foot we have
یا نه. موجودی‌ها را بررسی می‌کنم.
yaa na mojudihaa raa barresi mikonam
or no inventories D.O. I check

(248) **I don't like baths, I prefer showers.**
حمام کردن را دوست ندارم، دوش گرفتن را
hammaam kardan raa dust nadaaram dush gereftan raa
bathing D.O. I don't like showering D.O.
ترجیح می‌دهم.
tarjih midaham
I prefer

(249) **I don't allow my kids to watch TV for more than thirty minutes per day.**

من به بچه‌هایم اجازه نمی‌دهم که بیشتر از سی دقیقه در روز تلویزیون تماشا کنند.

man be bachchehaayam ejaaze nemidaham ke bishtar az si daqiqe dar ruz televiziyun tamaashaa konand.

I to my kids permission I don't give that more than thirty minute in day television they can watch

(250) **I don't doubt that you're right, but you still have to convince everyone else.**

من شک ندارم که حق با شماست. اما شما باید افراد دیگر را قانع کنید.

man shak nadaaraam ke haq baa shomaast. ammaa shomaa baayad afraad_e digar raa qaane' konid.

I doubt I don't have that right with (it is) you. but you must people other D.O. convince you do

(251) **I don't earn enough money to afford a new car.**

من آنقدر درآمد ندارم که بتوانم یک ماشین جدید بخرم.

man aanqadr daraamad nadaaram ke betavaanam yek maashin_e jadid bekharam.

I that much income I don't have that I could a car new I can buy

(252) **I don't feel well. I think I have a fever.**

حالم خوب نیست. فکر کنم تب دارم.

haalam khub nist. fekr konam tab daaram.

my state good it is not. I may think fever I have

(253) **I don't have a landline, but I have a cell phone.**

من تلفن ثابت ندارم، اما تلفن همراه دارم.

man telefon_e saabet nadaaram, ammaa telefon_e hamraah daaram.

I telephone fixed I don't have, but cell phone I have

(254) **I don't have an apartment yet. I'm living with a friend for the time being.**

من هنوز آپارتمان ندارم. فعلاً با دوستم زندگی می‌کنم.

man hanuz aapaartemaan nadaaram. fe'lan baa dustam zendegi mikonam.

I still apartment I don't have. currently with my friend I live

(255) **I don't have kids yet, but I hope to eventually have three.**

هنوز بچه ندارم، اما امیدوارم در نهایت سه تا داشته باشم.

hanuz bachche nadaaram, ammaa omidvaaram dar nahaayat se taa daashte baasham.

still kid I don't have, but I'm hopeful eventually three I may have

(256) **I don't know that word. I should look it up in a dictionary.**

من معنی این کلمه را نمی‌دانم. باید معنی آن را
man ma'ni_ye in kalame raa nemidaanam. baayad ma'ni_ye aan raa
I meaning this word D.O. I don't know must meaning that D.O.

در دیکشنری پیدا کنم.
dar dikshenri peydaa konam.
at dictionary I should find

(257) **I don't mind if you use the car today.**

مشکلی ندارم اگر امروز از ماشین استفاده کنی.
moshkeli nadaaram agar emruz az maashin estefaade koni.
problem I don't have if today from car you would use

(258) **I don't ride my motorcycle when it is this cold.**

وقتی هوا اینقدر سرد باشد، سوار موتورسیکلتم
vaqti havaa inqadr sard baashad, savaar_e motorsikletam
when weather this much cold it may be ride→ my motorcycle

نمی‌شوم.
nemishavam
I don't become →

(259) **I don't think you'll get that much money for the car. That is not realistic.**

فکر نمی‌کنم شما پول زیادی بابت این ماشین
fekr nemikonam shomaa pul_e ziyaadi baabat_e in maashin
I don't think you money much for this car

بدست آورید. واقع‌بینانه نیست.
bedast aavarid. vaaqebinaane nist.
you would get realistic it is not

(260) **I don't understand the humor of this comedian.**

من طنز این کمدین را متوجه نمی‌شوم.
man tanz_e in komediyan raa motevajjeh nemishavam.
I humor this comedian D.O. I don't understand

(261) **I don't understand what I can't explain.**

چیزی را که نتوانم توضیح بدهم،
chizi raa ke natavaanam tozih bedaham,
something D.O. that I may not be able explanation I can give

متوجه نمی‌شوم.
motevajjeh nemishavam.
I don't understand

(262) **I don't understand what you're saying. Can you please say it again more simply?**

متوجه نمی‌شوم چه می‌گویی. می‌توانی لطفاً دوباره آن
motevajjeh nemishavam che miguyi. mitavaani lotfan dobaare aan
I don't understand what you say you can please again that

را ساده‌تر بیان کنی؟
raa saadetar bayaan koni?
D.O. simpler you may state

(263) I don't want a job that makes me work on the weekend.

من شغلی نمی‌خواهم که مجبورم کند که آخر هفته‌ها کار کنم.

aakhar_e haftehaa	ke	majburam konad	ke	nemikhaaham	shoqli	man
weekends	that	it forces me	that	I don't want	a job	I

kaar konam
I would work

(264) I eat an apple every day with my breakfast.

من هر روز با صبحانه، یک سیب می‌خورم.

mikhoram	sib	yek	sobhaane	baa	ruz	har	man
I eat	apple	an	breakfast	with	day	every	I

(265) I exercise a lot and eat a lot of vegetables.

زیاد ورزش می‌کنم و سبزیجات زیادی می‌خورم.

mikhoram	ziyaadi	sabzijaat_e	va	varzesh mikonam	ziyaad
I eat	a lot	vegetables	and	I exercise	a lot

(266) I find this chair to be very uncomfortable.

به نظرم این صندلی اصلاً راحت نیست.

nist	raahat	aslan	sandali	in	nazaram	be
it is not	comfortable	at all	chair	this	my opinion	to

(267) I forgot my passport, so I had to quickly go back home to get it.

گذرنامه‌ام را فراموش کردم، بنابراین باید سریعاً به خانه برمی‌گشتم تا آن را بردارم.

be	sari'an	baayad	banaabarin	faraamush kardam	raa	gozarnaameam
to	quickly	had to	thus	I forgot	D.O.	my passport

bardaaram	raa	aan	taa	barmigashtam	khaane
I would pick up	D.O.	that	in order to	I was going back	home

(268) I forgot your birthday. I have quite a guilty conscience.

من تولدت را فراموش کردم. احساس گناه می‌کنم.

mikonam	gonaah	ehsaas_e	faraamush kardam	raa	tavallodat	man
I do	guilty	feeling	I forgot	D.O.	your birth	I

(269) I get along well with my daughter-in-law.

من با عروسم به خوبی کنار می‌آیم.

kenaar miaayam	be khubi	'arusam	baa	man
I get along	well	my daughter-in-law	with	I

(270) I get up every morning at six.

هر روز ساعت شش صبح، از خواب بلند می‌شوم.

boland mishavam	khaab	az	sobh	shesh_e	saa'at_e	ruz	har
I get up	sleep	from	morning	six	hour	day	every

(271) I go grocery shopping once a week.

من یک بار در هفته، به خرید خواربار می‌روم.

miravam	khaarobaar	kharid_e	be	hafte	dar	baar	yek	man
I go	groceries	buying	to	week	in	time	one	I

(272) I got married very young.

من وقتی خیلی جوان بودم، ازدواج کردم.
man vaqti kheyli javaan budam, ezdevaaj kardam
I when very young I was marriage I did

(273) I got the visa from the embassy.

من از سفارت، ویزا گرفتم.
man az sefaarat, vizaa gereftam
I from embassy visa I got

(274) I got you a gift. It's on the table.

من برایت یک هدیه گرفته‌ام. روی میز است.
man baraayat yek hediye gerefteam ru_ye miz ast
I for you a gift I have gotten on table it is

(275) I had an accident with the car. Now I have to report the damage to the insurance company.

با ماشینم تصادف کرده‌ام. حالا باید خسارت را به
baa maashinam tasaadof kardeam haalaa baayad khesaarat raa be
with my car accident I've done now must damage D.O. to

شرکت بیمه گزارش دهم.
sherkat_e bimeh gozaaresh daham
company insurance I should report

(276) I had great difficulty finding a parking space.

من در پیدا کردن جای پارک مشکل زیادی داشتم.
man dar peydaa kardan_e jaa_ye paark moshkel_e ziyaadi daashtam
I at finding place park difficulty great I had

(277) I had to wait a long time for an answer. But I got the job in the end.

باید برای دریافت پاسخ زمان زیادی
baayad baraaye daryaaft_e paasokh zamaan_e ziyaadi
must for reception answer time much

منتظر می‌ماندم. اما در نهایت، شغل را گرفتم.
montazer mimaandam ammaa dar nahaayat, shoql raa gereftam
I was waiting but in the end job D.O. I got

(278) I hate how my voice sounds.

از صدایم متنفرم.
az sedaayam motenafferam
from my voice I'm hateful

(279) I have a cavity in my tooth. I have to go to the dentist.

دندانم سوراخ شده است. باید به یک دندانپزشک
dandaanam suraakh shode ast baayad be yek dandaanpezeshk
my tooth cavity it has become must to a dentist

مراجعه کنم.
moraaje'e konam
I should refer

(280) I have a cold. I can't smell anything.	من سرما خورده‌ام. بوی هیچ چیزی را متوجه نمی‌شوم.	motevajjeh nemishavam raa hich chizi bu_ye khordeam sarmaa man / I don't understand D.O. nothing smell I have caught cold I
(281) I have a difficult week ahead of me. I have to work overtime every day.	هفته سختی را در پیش دارم. باید هر روز اضافه کاری کار کنم.	ruz har baayad daaram dar pish raa sakhti hafte_ye / day every must I have ahead D.O. hard week / kaar konam ezaafe kaari / I must work overtime
(282) I have a good relationship with my parents.	من رابطه خوبی با والدینم دارم.	daaram vaaledeynam baa khubi man raabete_ye / I have my parents with good my relationship
(283) I have a lot to do at the moment. – Then I don't want to disturb you any longer.	الان زیاد کار دارم. – پس نمی‌خواهم بیشتر از این مزاحم شما بشوم.	in az bishtar nemikhaaham pas daaram kaar ziyaad alaan / this than more I don't want so I have work a lot now / beshavam shomaa mozaahem_e / I would become you troublesome
(284) I have a small child and can't work eight hours a day. Therefore, I would like to work half-days.	من یک بچه کوچک دارم و نمی‌توانم هشت ساعت در روز کار کنم. بنابراین می‌خواهم نصف روز کار کنم.	hasht nemitavaanam va daaram kuchak bachche_ye yek man / eight I can't and I have small child a I / ruz nesf_e mikhaaham banaabarin kaar konam ruz dar saa'at / day half I want therefore I can work day per hour / kaar konam / I would work
(285) I have changed my mind. I am coming with you.	نظرم عوض شد. من با تو می‌آیم.	miaayam to baa man avaz shod nazaram / I come you with I it was changed my opinion
(286) I have injured myself. My hand is bleeding.	من به خودم صدمه زدم. از دستم خون می‌آید.	miaayad khun dastam az sadame zadam khodam be man / it is coming blood my hand from I injured myself to I
(287) I have many nice memories from my childhood.	من خاطرات خوب زیادی از کودکیم دارم.	daaram kudakiam az ziyaadi khub_e khaateraat_e man / I have my childhood from many good memories I

(288) I have no energy left for exercise in the evening.

عصرها دیگر انرژی‌ای برای ورزش کردن ندارم.

'asrhaa digar enerzhiiy baraaye varzesh kardan nadaaram
evenings anymore energy for exercising I don't have

(289) I have ten years of experience in this field.

من ده سال تجربه در این زمینه دارم.

man dah saal tajrobe dar in zamine daaram
I ten year experience in this field I have

(290) I have three kids and have no time anymore for my hobbies.

من سه تا بچه دارم و دیگر وقتی برای سرگرمی‌های

man se taa bachche daaram va digar vaqti baraaye sargarmihaa_ye
I three kid I have and anymore time for hobbies

خودم ندارم.

khodam nadaaram
myself I don't have

(291) I have to charge my phone. The battery is empty.

باید تلفنم را شارژ کنم. باتریش خالی است.

baayad telefonam raa shaarzh konam baatriyash khaali ast
must my phone D.O. charge I must do its battery empty it is

(292) I have two copies of the book. Do you want one?

من دو نسخه از کتاب را دارم. یکی را می‌خواهی؟

man do noskhe az ketaab raa daaram yeki raa mikhaahi
I two copy of book D.O. I have one D.O. you want

(293) I haven't been able to move my arm since the operation.

از وقتی جراحی کرده‌ام، نمی‌توانم بازویم را

az vaqti jarraahi kardeam nemitavaanam baazuyam raa
since surgery I have done I can't my arm D.O.

حرکت بدهم.

harekat bedaham
I can move

(294) I haven't eaten anything all day, so I'm quite hungry.

تمام روز هیچ چیز نخورده‌ام، بنابراین خیلی گرسنه‌ام.

tamaam_e ruz hich chiz nakhordeam banaabarin kheyli gorsneam
all day nothing I haven't eaten so very I'm hungry

(295) I haven't seen you in ages, but you haven't changed at all.

مدت‌هاست که تو را ندیده‌ام، اما تو اصلاً

moddathaast ke to raa nadideam ammaa to aslan
(it is) a long time that you D.O I haven't seen but you at all

تغییر نکرده‌ای.

taqiyr nakardeiy
you haven't changed

(296) I hit a big tree with my car. The tree is fine, but my car is destroyed.

با ماشینم به یک درخت بزرگ زدم. درخت سالم
baa maashinam be yek derakht_e bozorg zadam. derakht_e saalem
with my car to a big tree I hit tree fine

است، اما ماشین من داغان شد.
ast, ammaa maashin_e man daaqaan shod.
it is but my car destroyed it became

(297) I hope you haven't been waiting long.

امیدوارم زیاد منتظر نمانده باشید.
omidvaaram ziyaad montazer namaande baashid.
I hope very waiting you would have not stayed

(298) I immediately recognized my mother by her voice.

من بلافاصله مادرم را از روی صدایش
man belaafaasele maadaram raa az ru_ye sedaayash
I immediately my mother D.O. from her voice

تشخیص دادم.
tashkhis daadam.
I recognized

(299) I injured my knee. Now I can't run.

زانویم را زخمی کردم. حالا نمی‌توانم بدوم.
zaanuyam raa zakhmi kardam. haalaa nemitavaanam bedavam.
my knee D.O. wounded I did now I can't I can run

(300) I just need to quickly get some cash from the ATM.

باید سریع از دستگاه خودپرداز مقداری پول بگیرم.
baayad sari' az dastgaah_e khodpardaaz meqdaari pul begiram.
must quickly from ATM some money I should get

(301) I know a bit about dinosaurs, but I'm not an expert.

من کمی دربارهٔ داینا‌سورها می‌دانم، اما متخصص
man kami darbaare_ye daaynaasorhaa midaanam, ammaa motekhasses
I a little about dinosaurs I know but expert

نیستم.
nistam.
I'm not

(302) I learned so much before the exam. Afterwards I forgot almost everything.

من قبل از امتحان خیلی چیزها یاد گرفتم. پس از آن
man qabl az emtehaan kheyli chizhaa yaad gereftam. pas az aan
I before exam very things I learned after that

تقریباً همه چیز را فراموش کردم.
taqriban hame chiz raa faraamush kardam.
almost everything D.O. I forgot

(303) I left my luggage in a locker at the train station.

بار و بنه‌ام را در قفسه‌ی ایستگاه قطار جا گذاشتم.

man — I / baar o boneam — my luggage / raa — D.O. / dar — in / qafase_ye — locker / istgaah_e — station / qataar — train / jaa gozaashtam — I left

(304) I like listening to folk music on the radio.

من دوست دارم از رادیو به موسیقی محلی گوش بدهم.

man — I / dust daaram — I like / az — on / raadio — radio / be — to / musiqi_ye — music / mahalli — folk / gush bedaham — I would listen

(305) I like playing tennis, squash, and any other racquet sport.

من بازی تنیس، اسکواش و هر ورزش راکتی دیگر را دوست دارم.

man — I / baazi_ye — game / tenis — tennis / eskwaash — squash / va — and / har — every / varzesh_e — sport / raaketi — racquet / digar — other / raa — D.O. / dust daaram — I like

(306) I like to eat bread with honey and butter for breakfast.

دوست دارم برای صبحانه نان با عسل و کره بخورم.

dust daaram — I like / baraaye — for / sobhaane — breakfast / naan — bread / baa — with / 'asal — honey / va — and / kare — butter / bokhoram — I would eat

(307) I like to listen to music on the radio while I'm driving.

دوست دارم در هنگام رانندگی به موسیقی‌های رادیو گوش دهم.

dust daaram — I like / dar hengaam_e — while / raanandegi — driving / be — to / musiqihaa_ye — music / raadio — radio / gush daham — I would listen

(308) I lost fifteen percent of my body weight over the last year.

در طول سال گذشته، پانزده درصد از وزن بدنم را کم کردم.

dar — at / tul_e — during / saal_e — year / gozashte — past / paanzdah — fifteen / darsad — percentage / az — from / vazn_e — weight / badanam — my body / raa — D.O. / kam kardam — I reduced

(309) I lost my shoes when my feet sank into the mud.

وقتی که پایم به داخل گل و لای فرو رفت، کفشم را گم کردم.

vaqti — when / ke — that / paayam — my feet / be — to / daakhel_e — inside / gel o laay — mud / foru raft — it sank / kafsham — my shoe / raa — D.O. / gom kardam — I lost

(310) I lost my wedding ring while swimming in the lake.

حلقه ازدواجم را در هنگام شنا کردن در دریاچه گم کردم.

halqe_ye ezdevaajam raa dar hengaam_e shenaa kardan dar daryaache gom kardam
ring my marriage D.O. while swimming at lake I lost

(311) I love my family even though they drive me crazy most of the time.

من عاشق خانواده‌ام هستم، هر چند که بیشتر وقت‌ها دیوانه‌ام می‌کنند.

man aasheq_e khaanevaadeam hastam, har chand ke bishtar_e vaqthaa divaaneam mikonand
I I love my family I am even though that most times they drive me crazy

(312) I measured the room. It is exactly 20 m².

من اتاق را اندازه گرفتم. دقیقاً بیست متر مربع است.

man otaaq raa andaaze gereftam. daqiqan bist metr_e morabba' ast
I room D.O. I measured exactly twenty meter square it is

(313) I missed the train, but another one is coming in twenty minutes.

من از قطار جا ماندم، اما بیست دقیقه بعد، یکی دیگر می‌آید.

man az qataar jaa maandam, ammaa bist daqiqe ba'd, yeki digar miaayad
I from train I missed but twenty minute next one other it comes

(314) I need some good hand cream because my hands are so dry.

مقداری کرم دست خوب نیاز دارم، چون دست‌هایم خیلی خشک است.

meqdaari kerem_e dast_e khub niyaaz daaram, chon dasthaayam kheyli khoshk ast
some cream hand good I need because my hands very dry it is

(315) I need to pick up my daughter from school no later than three o'clock.

من باید حداکثر تا ساعت سه، دخترم را از مدرسه بردارم.

man baayad hadeaksar taa saa'at_e se, dokhtaram raa az madrese bardaaram
I must maximum until hour three my daughter D.O. from school I should pickup

38

(316) I need to take the car into the shop to get fixed.

باید ماشینم را برای تعمیر به مغازه ببرم.

baayad maashinam raa baraaye ta'miyr be maqaaze bebaram
must my car D.O. for repair to shop I should take

(317) I only buy organic fruit and vegetables.

من فقط میوه و سبزیجات ارگانیک می‌خرم.

man faqat mive va sabzijaat_e orgaanik mikharam
I only fruit and vegetables organic I buy

(318) I only just arrived. Do you mind if I use the toilet before we start chatting?

من تازه رسیده‌ام. اشکالی ندارد قبل از صحبت کردن، از دستشویی استفاده کنم؟

man taaze resideam eshkaali nadaarad qabl az
I recently I have arrived problem it doesn't have before

sohbat kardan az dastshuiy estefaade konam
talking from toilet I may use

(319) I plan to retire at the end of the year.

برنامه دارم در پایان سال بازنشسته شوم.

barnaame daaram dar paayaan_e saal baazneshaste shavam
plan I have at end year retired I would become

(320) I put only butter on my bread.

من فقط کره روی نان خود می‌گذارم.

man faqat kare ru_ye naan_e khod migozaaram
I only butter on bread self I put

(321) I ran as fast as I could, but I still missed the bus.

تا آنجا که توانستم سریع دویدم، اما باز هم از اتوبوس جا ماندم.

taa aanjaa ke tavaanestam sari' davidam ammaa baaz ham az
up to there that I could fast I ran but still too from

otobus jaa maandam
bus I stayed back

(322) I rang the doorbell, but nobody was at home.

زنگ در را زدم، اما کسی خانه نبود.

zang_e dar raa zadam ammaa kasi khaane nabud
bell door D.O. I hit but somebody home s/he was not

(323) I really enjoy this job, despite the low pay.

من از این کار، با وجود دستمزد کمش، واقعاً لذت می‌برم.

man az in kaar baa vojud_e dastmozd_e kamash vaaqe'an
I from this job with existence salary it's low really

lezzat mibaram
I enjoy

(324) **I really like Japanese cuisine.**
من غذاهای ژاپنی را خیلی دوست دارم.
man / qazaahaa_ye / zhaaponi / raa / kheyli / dust daaram
I / foods / Japanese / D.O. / very much / I like

(325) **I searched everywhere, but I can't find my sunglasses.**
من همه جا را گشتم، اما نمی‌توانم عینک آفتابیم را پیدا کنم.
man / hame / jaa / raa / gashtam / ammaa / nemitavaanam / eynak_e aaftaabiyam / raa / peydaa konam
I / every / place / D.O. / I searched / but / I can't / my sunglasses / D.O. / I can find

(326) **I should clean up before the guests arrive.**
بهتر است قبل از رسیدن مهمان‌ها نظافت کنم.
behtar / ast / qabl az / residan_e / mehmaanhaa / nezaafat konam
better / it is / before / arriving / guests / I should clean

(327) **I slipped because the floor is slippery.**
چون زمین لیز بود، سر خوردم.
chon / zamin / liz / bud / sor khordam
because / earth / slippery / it was / I slipped

(328) **I sold our old car and bought a new one.**
ماشین قدیمی‌مان را فروختم و یک جدیدش را خریدم.
maashin_e / qadimiyemaan / raa / forukhtam / va / yek / jadidash / raa / kharidam
car / our old / D.O. / I sold / and / a / its new / D.O. / I bought

(329) **I still have to pack my suitcase for the trip.**
هنوز باید چمدانم را برای سفر ببندم.
hanuz / baayad / chamedaanam / raa / baraaye / safar / bebandam
still / must / my suitcase / D.O. / for / travel / I should pack

(330) **I still live with my parents.**
من هنوز با پدر و مادرم زندگی می‌کنم.
man / hanuz / baa / pedar / o / maadaram / zendegi mikonam
I / still / with / father / and / my mother / I live

(331) **I talk to my mother every day.**
هر روز با مادرم صحبت می‌کنم.
har / ruz / baa / maadaram / sohbat mikonam
every / day / with / my mother / I talk

(332) **I think about many things differently now than before I had children.**
الان نسبت به قبل از بچه‌دار شدن، دربارۀ بسیاری از چیزها متفاوت فکر می‌کنم.
alaan / nesbat / be / qabl az / bachchedaar shodan / darbaare_ye / besyaari / az / chizhaa / motefavvet / fekr mikonam
now / relative / to / before / to have a baby / about / many / of / things / different / I think

(333) I think he is telling the truth, but I'm not completely sure.

فکر می‌کنم حقیقت را می‌گوید، اما کاملاً مطمئن نیستم.

fekr mikonam haqiqat raa miguyad, ammaa kaamelan motma'en nistam.

I think — truth — D.O. — he says — but — completely — sure — I'm not

(334) I think I made a good impression at the job interview.

فکر می‌کنم در مصاحبه‌ی کاری تأثیر خوبی گذاشتم.

fekr mikonam dar mosaahebe_ye kaari tasir_e khubi gozaashtam.

I think — at — interview — job — impression — good — I put

(335) I think the movie was good. What do you think?

به نظرم فیلم خوبی بود. شما چه فکر می‌کنید؟

be nazaram film_e khubi bud. shomaa che fekr mikonid?

to — my view — movie — good — it was — you — what — you think

(336) I thought that we could drive together and split the cost of gas.

من فکر کردم که می‌توانیم با هم رانندگی کنیم و هزینه‌ی بنزین را نصف کنیم.

man fekr kardam ke mitavaanim baa ham raanandegi konim va hazine_ye benzin raa nesf konim.

I — I thought — that — we can — with each other — we can drive — and — cost — gas — D.O. — we can split

(337) I understand you better when you don't speak in dialect.

وقتی با لهجه حرف نمی‌زنید، بهتر متوجه حرف‌هایتان می‌شوم.

vaqti baa lahje harf nemizanid, behtar motevajjeh harfhaayetaan mishavam.

when — in — dialect — you don't speak — better — ←understand — your speech — I become→

(338) I used to babysit him when he was a baby.

وقتی که او بچه بود، پرستارش بودم.

vaqti ke u bachche bud, parastaarash budam.

when — that — he — baby — he was — his babysitter (lit: nurse) — I was

(339) I used to be unemployed, but I recently got a job.

قبلاً بیکار بودم، اما به تازگی کاری پیدا کرده‌ام.

qablan bikaar budam, ammaa be taazegi kaari peydaa kardeam.

before — unemployed — I was — but — recently — a job — I have found

(340) I used to live in the city, but now I live in the suburbs with my family.

قبلاً در شهر زندگی می‌کردم، اما حالا در حومه شهر
qablan dar shahr zendegi mikardam, ammaa haalaa dar hume_ye shahr
before in city I was living but now at around city

به همراه خانواده‌ام زندگی می‌کنم.
be hamraah_e khaanevaadeam zendegi mikonam.
with along my family I live

(341) I usually wake up before my husband.

من معمولاً قبل از شوهرم از خواب بیدار می‌شوم.
man ma'mulan qabl az shoharam az khaab bidaar mishavam.
I usually before my husband from sleep I wake up

(342) I visited England for the first time five years ago.

پنج سال پیش، برای اولین بار، انگلستان را دیدم.
panj saal_e pish, baraaye avvalin baar, engelestaan raa didam.
five year ago for first time England D.O. I saw

(343) I want to take the advantage of the nice weather and go for a long walk.

می‌خواهم از هوای خوب استفاده کنم و به پیاده‌روی
mikhaaham az havaa_ye khub estefaade konam va be piyaaderavi_ye
I want from air good I would use and to walking

طولانی بروم.
tulaani beravam.
long I would go

(344) I want to be alone.

می‌خواهم تنها باشم.
mikhaaham tanhaa baasham.
I want alone I would be

(345) I want to clean the apartment thoroughly before our visitor arrives.

می‌خواهم قبل از رسیدن مهمانمان، آپارتمان را
mikhaaham qabl az residan_e mehmaanemaan, aapaartemaan raa
I want before arriving our guest apartment D.O.

کاملاً تمیز کنم.
kaamelan tamiz konam.
completely I would clean

(346) I want to exchange this shirt for a smaller size. This one is too big.

می‌خواهم این پیراهن را با سایز کوچک‌تر عوض کنم.
mikhaaham in piraahan raa baa saayz_e kuchektar avaz konam.
I want this shirt D.O. with size smaller I would change

این خیلی بزرگ است.
in kheyli bozorg ast.
this very big it is

(347) I want to go on an inexpensive vacation. What do you advise?

یک تعطیلات ارزان می‌خواهم. چه توصیه‌ای دارید؟
yek ta'tilaat_e arzaan mikhaaham. che tosiyeiy daarid
a vacation cheap I want what advice you have

(348) I was at the store the other day and ran into an old friend.

من آن روز در فروشگاه بودم و یک دوست قدیمی را
man aan ruz dar forushgaah budam va yek dust_e qadimi raa
I that day at store I was and a friend old D.O.

دیدم.
didam
I saw

(349) I was in a car accident, but it wasn't my fault.

من یک تصادف رانندگی داشتم، اما تقصیر من نبود.
man yek tasaadof_e raanandegi daashtam, ammaa taqsir_e man nabud
I a accident driving I had but my fault it was not

(350) I was just about to call you.

همین الان می‌خواستم با شما تماس بگیرم.
hamin alaan mikhaastam baa shomaa tamaas begiram
just now I was wanting with you I would call

(351) I was not happy with my job and quit.

از شغلم راضی نبودم و آن را ترک کردم.
az shoqlam raazi nabudam va aan raa tark kardam
from my job satisfied I was not and that D.O. I left

(352) I was sick yesterday, which is why I wasn't in the office.

دیروز مریض بودم و به همین دلیل در دفتر نبودم.
diruz mariz budam va be hamin dalil dar daftar nabudam
yesterday sick I was and for this reason in office I was not

(353) I was very happy to see you. Please visit again soon.

خیلی از دیدنت خوشحال شدم. لطفاً به زودی دوباره
kheyli az didanat khoshhaal shodam lotfan be zudi dobaare
very from seeing you happy I became please soon again

سر بزن.
sar bezan
stop by

(354) I weigh too much. I should lose weight.

وزنم خیلی زیاد است. باید وزن کم کنم.
vaznam kheyli ziyaad ast baayad vazn kam konam
my weight very much it is must weight I should lose

(355) I will be there in five minutes.

پنج دقیقه دیگر آنجا خواهم بود.
panj daqiqe_ye digar aanjaa khaaham bud
five minute other there I will be

(356) **I will copy the files to the flash drive for you.**
من فایل‌ها را برای شما در فلش کپی می‌کنم.
man faaylhaa raa baraaye shomaa dar felash kopi mikonam
I / files / D.O. / for / you / at / flash (drive) / I copy

(357) **I will definitely help you. You can count on me.**
حتماً به تو کمک خواهم کرد. می‌توانی روی من
hatman be to komak khaaham kard. mitavaani ru_ye man
definitely / to / you / I will help / you can / on / I

حساب کنی.
hesaab koni
you can count

(358) **I will give you another chance.**
یک فرصت دیگر به تو می‌دهم.
yek forsat_e digar be to midaham
a / chance / another / to / you / I give

(359) **I will never be able to forgive him for what he did.**
هیچ وقت نمی‌توانم او را برای کاری که کرد ببخشم.
hich vaqt nemitavaanam u raa baraaye kaari ke kard bebakhsham
never / I can't / him / for / job / that / he did / I can forgive

(360) **I will never come back to this restaurant.**
من هرگز دیگر به این رستوران نمی‌آیم.
man hargez digar be in resturaan nemiaayam
I / never / again / to / this / restaurant / I don't come

(361) **I won't let you treat me like this anymore.**
دیگر اجازه نمی‌دهم اینطوری با من رفتار کنی.
digar ejaaze nemidaham intowri baa man raftaar koni
no longer / I don't allow / this way / with / I / you would behave

(362) **I work part-time while also going to university.**
همزمان با تحصیل در دانشگاه، نیمه وقت هم
hamzamaan baa tahsil dar daaneshgaah, nime vaqt ham
simultaneous / with / studying / at / university / part-time / also

کار می‌کنم.
kaar mikonam
I work

(363) **I would like more information before I make a decision.**
قبل از تصمیم‌گیری اطلاعات بیشتری می‌خواستم.
qabl az tasmim giri ettelaa'aat_e bishtari mikhaastam
before / decision-making / information / more / I was wanting

(364) I would like to come, but unfortunately I can't.

دوست داشتم بیایم، اما متأسفانه نمی‌توانم.

dust dashtam	biyaayam	ammaa	moteassefaane	nemitavaanam
I liked	I would come	but	unfortunately	I can't

(365) I would like to eat something before we go.

می‌خواستم قبل از رفتن چیزی بخورم.

mikhaastam	qabl az	raftan	chizi	bokhoram
I was wanting	before	going	something	I would eat

(366) I would like to lose weight. Therefore, I'm going on a diet.

می‌خواستم وزنم را کم کنم. بنابراین می‌خواهم رژیم غذایی بگیرم.

mikhaastam	vaznam	raa	kam konam	banaabarin	mikhaaham
I was wanting	my weight	D.O.	I would reduce	thus	I want

rezhim_e	qazaaiy	begiram
regimen	food	I would take

(367) I would like to work in an office instead of outside under the hot sun.

دوست داشتم به جای کار در فضای بیرون و زیر آفتاب داغ، در یک دفتر کار می‌کردم.

dust daashtam	be jaa_ye	kaar	dar	fazaa_ye	birun	va	zir_e
I liked	instead	working	at	space	outside	and	under

aaftaab_e	daaq	dar	yek	daftar	kaar mikardam
sun	hot	at	a	office	I was working

(368) If I were rich, I would go on a round-the-world trip.

اگر پولدار بودم، به یک سفر دور دنیا می‌رفتم.

agar	puldaar	budam	be	yek	safar_e	dowr_e	donyaa	miraftam
if	rich	I was	to	a	travel	around	world	I was going

(369) If it rains, we'll just have the party at our house instead of at the park.

اگر باران بیاید، ما به جای پارک، مهمانی را در خانه‌مان برگزار می‌کنیم.

agar	baaraan	biyaayad	maa	be jaa_ye	paark	mehmaani	raa	dar
if	rain	it may come	we	instead	park	party	D.O.	at

khaanamaan	bargozaar mikonim
our house	we hold

(370) If it's supposed to rain, then you should bring an umbrella.

اگر قرار است باران ببارد، بهتر است چتر ببرید.

agar	qaraar	ast	baaraan	bebaarad	behtar	ast	chatr	bebarid
if	assume	it is	rain	it may pour	better	it is	umbrella	you should take

(371) If the strawberries have gone bad, then you should throw them away.	اگر توت فرنگی خراب شده است، باید آنها را دور بیندازید.	agar tut farangi kharaab shode ast, baayad aanhaa raa dur biyandaazid. / if strawberry bad it has become, must them D.O. away you should throw
(372) If the weather is nice, we could have a picnic.	اگر هوا خوب باشد، می‌توانیم به پیک‌نیک برویم.	agar havaa khub baashad, mitavaanim be piknik beravim. / if weather good it may be, we can to picnic we can go
(373) If we hurry, we can still watch the end of the game.	اگر عجله کنیم، هنوز هم می‌رسیم آخر بازی را تماشا کنیم.	agar 'ajale konim, hanuz ham miresim aakhar_e baazi raa tamaashaa konim. / if we would hurry, still too we arrive end game D.O. we can watch
(374) If you do not pay the bill on time, you will receive an overdue notice.	اگر قبض را به موقع پرداخت نکنی، یک اخطار برای تاخیر دریافت می‌کنی.	agar qabz raa be moqe' pardaakht nakoni, yek ekhtaar baraaye takhiyr daryaaft mikoni. / if bill D.O. at time you would not pay, a warning for delay you may receive
(375) If you drive drunk, you will go to jail.	اگر در حال مستی رانندگی کنی به زندان می‌روی.	agar dar haal_e masti raanandegi koni be zendaan miravi. / if at condition drunk you would drive to prison you go
(376) If you have any questions, go to the information desk.	اگر سؤالی دارید، به قسمت اطلاعات بروید.	agar soaali daarid, be qesmat_e ettelaa'aat beravid. / if a question you have, to section information go
(377) If you have low income, you only pay a little tax.	اگر درآمدتان کم باشد، مالیات کمی پرداخت خواهید کرد.	agar daraamadetaan kam baashad, maaliyaat_e kami pardaakht khaahid kard. / if your income low it may be, tax low you will pay
(378) If you press here, the door opens.	اگر اینجا را فشار دهید، در باز می‌شود.	agar injaa raa feshaar dahid, dar baaz mishavad. / if here D.O. you would press, door open it becomes

1000 Sentences

(379) If you spend more than you earn, then you won't save any money.

اگر بیش از درآمدتان پول خرج کنید، نمی‌توانید هیچ
agar bish az daraamadetaan pul kharj konid, nemitavaanid hich
if more than your income money you would spend you can't no

پولی پس‌انداز کنید.
puli pasandaaz konid
money you can save

(380) If you want to open the file you have to click twice with the mouse.

اگر می‌خواهید فایل را باز کنید، باید با موس
agar mikhaahid faayl raa baaz konid, baayad baa mos
if you want file D.O. you would open must with mouse

دو بار کلیک کنید.
do baar kelik konid
twice you should click

(381) I'll be right back. This should take only a few minutes.

همین الان بر می‌گردم. تنها چند دقیقه طول می‌کشد.
hamin alaan bar migardam. tanhaa chand daqiqe tul mikeshad
just now I come back only several minute it takes (time)

(382) I'll call you tonight.

امشب با شما تماس می‌گیرم.
emshab baa shomaa tamaas migiram
tonight with you I call

(383) I'll email you when I get there once I have internet access.

وقتی آنجا برسم به محض دسترسی به اینترنت به
vaqti aanjaa beresam be mahz_e dastresi be internet be
when there I would arrive as soon as accessing to internet to

شما ایمیل می‌زنم.
shomaa imeyl mizanam
you I email

(384) I'll get you something to drink. You must be thirsty.

برایتان نوشیدنی می‌آورم. باید تشنه باشید.
baraayetaan nushidani miaavaraam. baayad teshne baashid
for you beverage I bring must thirsty you should be

(385) I'll give this to you for free. - Why? What's the catch?

این را مجانی به تو می‌دهم. - چرا؟ مشکلش چیست؟
in raa majjaani be to midaham. cheraa moshkelash chist
this D.O. free to you I give why its problem what is it

(386) I'll meet you at the cafe across from the school.

شما را در کافه، رو به روی مدرسه خواهم دید.
shomaa raa dar kaafe, ru be ru_ye madrese khaaham did
you D.O. at cafe across from school I will see

47

(387) I'll sell you the tomatoes for half price.

من گوجه فرنگی را به نصف قیمت به شما می‌فروشم.
miforusham shomaa be qeymat nesf_e be raa goje farangi man
I sell you to price half to D.O. tomato I

(388) I'll shovel the snow out of the driveway if you shovel the sidewalk.

اگر تو پیاده‌رو را پارو کنی، من برف را از جلوی
jelo_ye az raa barf man paaru koni raa piyaadero to agar
front from D.O. snow I you would shovel D.O. sidewalk you if

خانه با پارو کنار می‌زنم.
kenaar mizanam paaru baa khaane
I pull aside shovel with house

(389) I'll take you home.

من شما را به خانه‌تان می‌رسانم.
miresaanam khaanetan be shomaa raa man
I take your home to you I

(390) I'll transfer the money to you electronically.

من پول را به صورت الکترونیکی برایت منتقل می‌کنم.
montaqel mikonam baraayat elekteroniki surat_e be raa pul man
I transfer for you electronic form to D.O. money I

(391) I'll wait for you in the car.

من توی ماشین منتظرتم.
montazeretam maashin tu_ye man
I'm waiting for you car inside I

(392) I'm already looking forward to my next vacation.

من از حالا مشتاقانه منتظر تعطیلات بعدیم هستم.
hastam ba'diyam ta'tilaat_e montazer_e moshtaaqaane haalaa az man
I am my next vacation anticipating eagerly now from I

(393) I'm doing an internship at a company for three months this summer.

تابستان امسال به مدت سه ماه در یک شرکت،
sherkat yek dar maah se moddat_e be emsaal taabestaan_e
company a at month three duration for this year summer

کارآموزی می‌کنم.
mikonam kaaraamuzi
I do internship

(394) I'm feel better today, but yesterday I was in a really bad mood.

امروز حالم بهتر است، اما دیروز واقعاً روحیه
ruhiyye_ye vaaqe'an diruz ammaa ast behtar haalam emruz
mood really yesterday but it is better my mood today

بدی داشتم.
dashtam badi
I had bad

I'm going out with my sisters tonight.	امشب با خواهرهایم بیرون می‌روم. *miravam birun khaaharhaayam baa emshab* I go out my sisters with tonight	(395)
I'm happy that everything went so well.	خوشحالم که همه چیز خوب پیش رفت. *pish raft khub hame chiz ke khoshhaalam* it progressed well everything that I'm happy	(396)
I'm learning Portuguese because I want to travel to Brazil.	من دارم زبان پرتغالی یاد می‌گیرم، چون می‌خواهم *mikhaaham chon yaad migiram porteqaali zabaan_e daaram man* I want because I learn → Portuguese language ← I am I به برزیل سفر کنم. *safar konam berezil be* I would travel Brazil to	(397)
I'm learning to play guitar. I practice an hour every day.	من دارم گیتار زدن یاد می‌گیرم. من هر روز یک *yek ruz har man yaad migiram zadan gitaar daaram man* one day every I I learn → playing guitar ← I am I ساعت تمرین می‌کنم. *tamrin mikonam saa'at* I practice hour	(398)
I'm looking for a car seat for my three-year-old son.	من به دنبال صندلی ماشین، برای پسر سه ساله‌ام *se saaleam pesar_e baraaye maashin sandali_ye be donbaal_e man* my three year old son for car seat ← looking for I می‌گردم. *migardam* I look →	(399)
I'm looking for a low-priced vacation home.	من به دنبال یک خانه‌ی ییلاقی ارزان قیمت می‌گردم. *migardam qeymat arzaan yeylaaqi_ye khaane_ye yek be donbaal_e man* I look → price cheap summer house a ← looking for I	(400)
I'm looking for a used car. It may not cost more than 3000 Euro.	دنبال یک ماشین دست دوم می‌گردم که قیمتش *qeymatash ke migardam dast_e dovvom maashin_e yek donbaal_e* its price that I look → secondhand car a ← in search of بیشتر از سه هزار یورو نباشد. *nabaashad yuro hezaar se az bishtar* it may not be Euro thousand three than more	(401)

49

(402)	I'm looking for an apartment with three bedrooms.	من به دنبال یک آپارتمان سه خوابه هستم. *man be donbaal_e yek aapaartemaan_e se khaabe hastam* I ←looking for a apartment three bedroom I am→
(403)	I'm not interested in philosophy, but I'm very interested in physics.	من به فلسفه علاقه‌ای ندارم، اما به فیزیک بسیار علاقه‌مندم. *man be falsafe 'alaaqeiy nadaaram, ammaa be fizik besyaar alaaqemandam* I to philosophy interest I don't have, but to physics very I'm interested
(404)	I'm on vacation until the end of August.	من تا آخر آگوست در تعطیلات هستم. *man taa aakhar_e aagost dar ta'tilaat hastam* I until end August in vacation I am
(405)	I'm out of money. May I borrow some?	پولم تمام شده است. می‌توانم کمی از شما قرض کنم؟ *pulam tamaam shode ast. mitavaanam kami az shomaa qarz konam* my money finished it has become. I can some from you I may borrow
(406)	I'm quite nervous. My heart is pounding.	کاملاً عصبی هستم. تپش قلب دارم. *kaamelan 'asabi hastam. tapesh_e qalb daaram* quite nervous I am. beating heart I have
(407)	I'm seriously considering whether I should move to another city.	من جدی در این فکر هستم که آیا باید به شهر دیگری نقل مکان کنم یا خیر. *man jeddi dar in fekr hastam ke aayaa baayad be shahr_e digari naql_e makaan konam yaa kheyr* I serious in this thought I am that I.P. must to city another move place I should do or not
(408)	I'm starting to doubt my boss's leadership skills.	من دارم به مهارت‌های رهبری رئیسم شک می‌کنم. *man daaram be mahaarathaa_ye rahbari_ye raiysam shak mikonam* I ←I am to skills leadership my boss I doubt→
(409)	I'm staying home until the package is delivered.	تا زمان تحویل بسته، در خانه می‌مانم. *taa zamaan_e tahvil_e baste dar khaane mimaanam* until time delivery package at home I stay

(410) **I'm used to waking up early because I have kids.**
من چون بچه دارم، عادت کرده‌ام زود بیدار شوم.
man chon bachche daaram, 'aadat kardeam zud bidaar shavam.
I because kid I have accustomed I have early I would wake up

(411) **I'm working from home today.**
امروز از خانه کار می‌کنم.
emruz az khaane kaar mikonam.
today from home I work

(412) **In autumn we gather mushrooms in the forest.**
در پاییز ما از جنگل قارچ جمع می‌کنیم.
dar paaiyz maa az jangal qaarch jam' mikonim.
at autumn we from forest mushroom we collect

(413) **In chess, each player has sixteen pieces.**
در شطرنج، هر بازیکن شانزده مهره دارد.
dar shatranj, har baazikon shaanzdah mohre daarad.
in chess each player sixteen piece s/he has

(414) **In general, I am very satisfied with my job.**
به طور کلی خیلی از شغلم راضی هستم.
be tor_e kolli kheyli az shoqlam raazi hastam.
generally very from my job satisfied I am

(415) **In Iceland there are only three hot days per year.**
در ایسلند فقط سه روز در سال هوا گرم است.
dar island faqat se ruz dar saal havaa garm ast.
in Iceland only three day in year weather warm it is

(416) **In my free time I am learning to play the violin.**
در وقت‌های آزادم، یاد می‌گیرم که چطور ویولون بزنم.
dar vaqthaa_ye aazaadam, yaad migiram ke chetowr viyolon bezanam.
in times my free I learn that how violin I would play

(417) **In my psychology class there are more women than men.**
در کلاس روان‌شناسیم، تعداد زنان بیشتر از مردان است.
dar kelaas_e ravaan shenaasiyam, te'daad_e zanaan bishtar az mardaan ast.
in class my psychology number women more than men it is

(418) **In order to vote, please go into this booth.**
برای رأی دادن، لطفاً وارد این اتاقک شوید.
baraaye ray daadan, lotfan vaared_e in otaaqak shavid.
for voting please ←enter this booth become→

(419) **In soccer, there are eleven players on the field for each team.**

در فوتبال، یازده بازیکن از هر تیم در زمین حضور دارند.

dar futbaal, yaazdah baazikon az har tim dar zamin hozur daarand.
in soccer/football eleven player from each team at field presence they have

(420) **In Spain it is common to eat late at night.**

در اسپانیا، دیر شام خوردن رایج است.

dar espaaniyaa, dir shaam khordan raayej ast.
in Spain late dinner eating common it is

(421) **In the summer you should not go out into the sun without wearing sunscreen.**

در تابستان بهتر است بدون زدن کرم ضد آفتاب، زیر آفتاب نروید.

dar taabestaan behtar ast bedun_e zadan_e kerem_e zedd_e aaftaab, zir_e aaftaab naravid.
in summer better it is without applying cream anti sun under sun don't go

(422) **In this market you can negotiate and get things cheaper.**

در این بازار می‌توانید چانه بزنید و چیزها را ارزان‌تر بخرید.

dar in baazaar mitavaanid chaane bezanid va chizhaa raa arzaantar bekharid.
in this market you can you can negotiate and things D.O. cheaper you would buy

(423) **Is the ring made of gold? - Sort of, it's gold-plated.**

آیا این حلقه از طلا ساخته شده است؟ - یه جورایی. روکش آن طلا است.

aayaa in halqe az talaa saakhte shode ast? ye juraayi. rukesh_e aan talaa ast.
I.P. this ring from gold it has been made sort of coating that gold it is

(424) **Is your cell phone broken? We'll send it back to the manufacturer and have it repaired.**

تلفن همراه شما خراب شده است؟ ما آن را برای تولید کننده می‌فرستیم تا تعمیرش کنند.

telefon_e hamraah_e shomaa kharaab shode ast? maa aan raa baraaye tolid konande miferestim taa ta'miyrash konand.
your cell phone broken it has become we that D.O. for manufacturer we send so they would repair it

(425) **It is better to give than to receive.**

دادن بهتر از گرفتن است.

daadan behtar az gereftan ast.
giving better than receiving it is

(426) It is cold outside.

بیرون سرد است.
birun sard ast
outside cold it is

(427) It is exactly eight o'clock.

دقیقاً ساعت هشت است.
daqiqan saa'at hasht ast
exactly hour eight it is

(428) It is so dark in this room. Where is the light switch?

این اتاق خیلی تاریک است. کلید برق کجاست؟
in otaaq kheyli taarik ast. kelid_e barq kojaast
this room very dark it is switch electricity where is it

(429) It is very kind of you to pick me up.

خیلی محبت کردی که دنبالم آمدی.
kheyli mohabbat kardi ke donbaalam aamadi
very kind you did that for me you came

(430) It just stopped raining, and now there is a rainbow.

همین الان باران افتاد و حالا رنگین کمان شده است.
hamin alaan baaraan oftaad va haalaa rangin kamaan shode ast
just now rain it stopped and now rainbow it has become

(431) It rained, so I don't need to water my garden.

باران آمد، بنابراین لازم نیست باغچه‌ام را آب بدهم.
baaraan aamad banaabarin laazem nist baaqcheam raa aab bedaham
rain it came so necessary it is not my garden D.O. water I would give

(432) It takes a lot of courage to start a new life in a foreign country.

شروع یک زندگی جدید در یک کشور خارجی، شجاعت زیادی می‌خواهد.
shoru'_e yek zendegi_ye jadid dar yek keshvar_e khaareji, shojaa'at_e ziyaadi mikhaahad
starting a life new in a country foreign courage much it requires

(433) It takes me about 10 minutes to drive to work.

باید حدود ده دقیقه رانندگی کنم تا به محل کار برسم.
baayad hodud_e dah daqiqe raanandegi konam taa be mahall_e kaar beresam
must about ten minute I should drive until to place work I would arrive

(434) It was a great concert. The audience was really enthusiastic.

کنسرت خیلی خوبی بود. حاضران واقعاً مشتاق بودند.
konsert_e kheyli khubi bud. haazeraan vaaqe'an moshtaaq budand.
concert very good it was. audience really enthusiastic they were

(435) It's strange that my brother isn't here yet. He is usually so punctual.

عجیب است که برادرم هنوز نیامده است. او معمولاً خیلی وقت‌شناس است.
'ajib ast ke baraadaram hanuz nayaamade ast. u ma'mulan kheyli vaqtshenaas ast.
strange it is that my brother still he has not come. he usually very punctual he is

(436) It's stuffy in here. Please open the window.

هوای اینجا کثیف است. لطفاً پنجره را باز کنید.
havaa_ye injaa kasif ast. lotfan panjere raa baaz konid.
weather here dirty it is. please window D.O. open

(437) I've been awake for two hours already.

من دو ساعت است که از خواب بیدار شده‌ام.
man do saa'at ast ke az khaab bidaar shodeam.
I two hour it is that from sleep awake I have become

(438) I've had a sore throat since yesterday.

من از دیروز گلودرد دارم.
man az diruz galudard daaram.
I since yesterday sore throat I have

(439) I've never heard that expression.

من تا حالا این عبارت را نشنیده‌ام.
man taa haalaa in ebaarat raa nashnideam.
I until now this phrase D.O. I have not heard

(440) Just ask my girlfriend. She always has good ideas.

از دوست دخترم بپرسید. او همیشه ایده‌های خوبی دارد.
az dust dokhtaram beporsid. u hamishe idehaa_ye khubi daarad.
from my girlfriend ask. she always ideas good she has

(441)	Karl is already over sixty. But he is still very fit.	کارل بالای شصت سال دارد، اما هنوز هم بسیار خوش‌اندام است.	karl baalaa_ye shast saal daarad, ammaa hanuz ham besyaar khoshandaam ast / Karl over sixty year he has but still too very fit body he is
(442)	Let me know as soon as possible, please.	لطفاً در اسرع وقت به من اطلاع دهید.	lotfan dar asra'_e vaqt be man ettelaa' dahid / please as soon as possible to I notify
(443)	Let's eat dinner on the balcony.	بیایید شام را در بالکن بخوریم.	biyaaiyd shaam raa dar baalkon bokhorim / come dinner D.O. at balcony we should eat
(444)	Look at the camera and smile!	به دوربین نگاه کنید و لبخند بزنید!	be durbin negaah konid va labkhand bezanid / to camera look and smile
(445)	Look both ways before crossing the street.	قبل از عبور از خیابان، هر دو طرف را نگاه کنید.	qabl az 'obur az khiyaabaan, har do taraf raa negaah konid / before crossing from street every two side D.O. look
(446)	Making mistakes is quite normal.	اشتباه کردن کاملاً طبیعی است.	eshtebaah kardan kaamelan tabi'i ast / mistake making completely natural it is
(447)	Many artists and musicians live in this neighborhood.	بسیاری از هنرمندان و نوازندگان در این محله زندگی می‌کنند.	besyaari az honarmandaan va navaazandegaan dar in mahalle zendegi mikonand / many from artists and musicians in this neighborhood they live
(448)	Many immigrants come from India.	خیلی از مهاجران از هند می‌آیند.	kheyli az mohaajeraan az hend miaayand / many of immigrants from India they come
(449)	Many words have several meanings.	بسیاری از کلمات، چندین معنی دارند.	besyaari az kalamaat, chandin ma'ni daarand / many of words several meaning they have
(450)	Marco speaks four languages.	مارکو به چهار زبان صحبت می‌کند.	maarko be chahaar zabaan sohbat mikonad / Marco to four language he speaks

(451) Maria is very intelligent and is very good at math.

ماریا بسیار باهوش و در ریاضی بسیار خوب است.

maariyaa besyaar baahush va dar riyaazi besyaar khub ast
Maria very smart and at math very good she is

(452) May I borrow your phone charger? My battery died.

آیا می‌توانم شارژر گوشیتان را قرض کنم؟

aayaa mitavaanam shaarzher_e gushiyetaan raa qarz konam
I.P. I can charger your phone D.O. I may borrow

باتری من تمام شده است.

baatri_ye man tamaam shode ast
my battery finished it has become

(453) Men and women have equal rights - at least they do in my country.

مردان و زنان حقوق برابری دارند - دست کم، در

mardaan va zanaan hoquq_e baraabari daarand dast_e kam dar
men and women rights equal they have at least in

کشور من اینگونه است.

keshvar_e man ingune ast
my country such it is

(454) Messi is a famous soccer player.

مسی بازیکن فوتبال معروفی است.

mesi baazikon_e futbaal_e ma'rufi ast
Messi player football/soccer famous he is

(455) Michael has been absent from school for three days.

مایکل سه روز از مدرسه غایب بوده است.

maaykel se ruz az madrese qaayeb bude ast
Michael three day from school absent he has been

(456) Mike has a beard now. He looks much older.

مایک حالا ریش دارد. او خیلی پیرتر به نظر می‌رسد.

maayk haalaa rish daarad u kheyli pirtar be nazar miresad
Mike now beard he has he very older he looks

(457) Mo drives his motorcycle to work every day.

مو هر روز با موتورسیکلتش به سر کار می‌رود.

mo har ruz baa motorsikletash be sar_e kaar miravad
Mo every day with his motorcycle to he goes to work

(458) Mom cut her finger while chopping garlic.

مامان در حین خرد کردن سیر انگشتش را برید.

maamaan dar heyn_e khord kardan_e sir angoshtash raa borid
mom while chopping garlic her finger D.O. she cut

(459) Monday is a national holiday.

دوشنبه تعطیل ملی است.

doshanbe ta'til_e melli ast
Monday holiday national it is

(460) More than two hundred guests are coming to the wedding.

بیش از دویست مهمان به عروسی می‌آیند.

bish az devist mehmaan be 'arusi miaayand
more than two hundred guest to wedding they come

1000 Sentences

(461) Most people don't realize that doctors usually aren't experts in nutrition.

بیشتر مردم متوجه نیستند که پزشکان معمولاً متخصص تغذیه نیستند.

bishtar_e mardom motevajjeh nistand ke pezeshkaan ma'mulan motekhasses_e taqziye nistand
most people they don't understand that doctors usually expert nutrition they are not

(462) Most scientists say climate change is the fault of humans.

بیشتر دانشمندان می‌گویند که انسان‌ها در تغییرات اقلیمی مقصر هستند.

bishtar_e daaneshmandaan miguyand ke ensaanhaa dar taqiyraat_e eqlimi moqasser hastand
most scientists they say that humans at changes climatic guilty they are

(463) My baby knows how to use a spoon.

بچه‌ی من، نحوه‌ی استفاده از قاشق را بلد است.

bachche_ye man nahve_ye estefaade az qaashoq raa balad ast
my baby how use from spoon D.O. s/he knows

(464) My boy used to love those toys, but he doesn't care about them anymore.

پسرم قبلاً عاشق این اسباب‌بازی‌ها بود، اما دیگر علاقه‌ای به آن‌ها ندارد.

pesaram qablan aasheq_e in asbaabbaazihaa bud ammaa digar 'alaaqeiy be aanhaa nadaarad
my son before loved this toys he was but anymore interest to they he doesn't have

(465) My brother is a very tidy person, while my sister is a slob.

برادرم شخص بسیار مرتبی است، در حالی که خواهرم شلخته است.

baraadaram shakhs_e besyaar morattabi ast dar haali ke khaaharam shelakhte ast
my brother person very tidy he is whereas my sister slob she is

(466) My brother is three years younger than me.

برادرم سه سال کوچک‌تر از من است.

baraadaram se saal kuchektar az man ast
my brother three year younger than I he is

(467) My brother never answers his phone when I call.

وقتی با برادرم تماس می‌گیرم، هیچ وقت تلفن را جواب نمی‌دهد.

vaqti baa baraadaram tamaas migiram hich vaqt telefon raa javaab nemidahad
when with my brother I call never telephone D.O. he doesn't answer

(468) **My car is brand new. I just bought it yesterday.**

ماشین من کاملاً جدید است. دیروز آن را خریدم.

kharidam | raa | aan | diruz | ast | jadid | kaamelan | maashin_e man
I bought | D.O. | it | yesterday | it is | new | completely | my car

(469) **My children are very diligent. They always do their homework right when they get home.**

فرزندان من بسیار کوشا هستند. آنها همیشه به محض

be mahz_e | hamishe | aanhaa | hastand | kushaa | besyaar | farzandaan_e man
as soon as | always | they | they are | diligent | very | my children

رسیدن به خانه تکالیف خود را انجام می‌دهند.

anjaam midahand | raa | khod | takaalif_e | khaane | be | residan
they do | D.O. | self | homework | home | at | arriving

(470) **My colleague strongly believes that he deserves a promotion.**

همکار من قویاً باور دارد که شایسته‌ی ترفیع شغلی

shoqli | tarfi'_e | shaayeste_ye | ke | baavar daarad | qaviyyan | hamkaar_e man
work | promotion | ←he deserves | that | he believes | strongly | my colleague

است.

ast
he is→

(471) **My daughter never wants my advice.**

دخترم نمی‌خواهد که من نصیحتش کنم.

nasihatash konam | man | ke | nemikhaahad | dokhtaram
I would advise her | I | that | she does not want | my daughter

(472) **My daughter starts high school next year.**

دخترم سال بعد به دبیرستان می‌رود.

miravad | dabirestaan | be | ba'd | saal_e | dokhtaram
she goes | high school | to | next | year | my daughter

(473) **My favorite drink is fresh-squeezed orange juice.**

نوشیدنی دلخواه من، آب پرتقال تازه است.

ast | taaze | porteqaal_e | aab | delkhaah_e man | nushidani_ye
it is | fresh | orange | water | my favorite | beverage

(474) **My flight was canceled because of bad weather.**

پروازم به دلیل بدی آب و هوا لغو شد.

laqv shod | aab o havaa | badi_ye | dalil_e | be | parvaazam
it was canceled | weather | bad | due | to | my flight

(475) **My girlfriend is a caregiver in a retirement home.**

دوست دختر من پرستار خانه‌ی سالمندان است.

ast | saalmandaan | khaane_ye | parastaar_e | dust dokhtar_e man
she is | elderly | home | nurse | my girlfriend

(476) **My grandfather is not working anymore. He is retired.**

پدربزرگم دیگر کار نمی‌کند. او بازنشسته است.

ast | baazneshaste | u | kaar nemikonad | digar | pedarbozorgam
he is | retired | he | he doesn't work | anymore | my grandfather

(477)	مادربزرگم دیگر نمی‌تواند از پله‌ها بالا برود. *maadarbozorgam digar nemitavaanad az pellehaa baalaa beravad* my grandmother anymore she can't from stairs she can climb	My grandma can't climb stairs anymore.
(478)	مادربزرگم تازه هشتاد و پنج ساله شده است. *maadarbozorgam taaze hashtaad o panj saal_e shode ast* my grandmother recently eighty and five year she has become	My grandma just turned 85.
(479)	مادربزرگم داستان‌های جالبی از جوانی خود، برای ما تعریف کرد. *maadarbozorgam daastaanhaa_ye jaalebi az javaani_ye khod baraaye maa ta'rif kard* my grandmother stories interesting from youth self for we she defined	My grandmother told us interesting stories of her youth.
(480)	پدربزرگ و مادربزرگ من سال‌ها پیش فوت کردند، اما هنوز هم می‌توانم آنها را به خوبی به یاد بیاورم. *pedarbozorg va maadarbozorg_e man saalhaa pish fot kardand ammaa hanuz ham mitavaanam aanhaa raa be khubi be yaad biyaavaram* grandfather and my grandmother years ago they died but still I can them well I can remember	My grandparents died many years ago, but I can still remember them well.
(481)	مادرم برای تولدش گل و شکلات گرفت. *maadaram baraaye tavallodash gol va shokolaat gereft* my mother for her birthday flower and chocolate she got	My mother got flowers and chocolate for her birthday.
(482)	مادر من بیست سال است که کسب و کار خودش را اداره می‌کند. *maadar_e man bist saal ast ke kasb o kaar_e khodash raa edaare mikonad* my mother twenty year it is that business herself D.O. she manages	My mother has been running her own business for twenty years.
(483)	خانواده‌ی مادرم بسیار بزرگ است، به همین دلیل، خاله‌ها و عموهای زیادی دارم. *khaanevaade_ye maadaram besyaar bozorg ast be hamin dalil khaalehaa va amuhaa_ye ziyaadi daaram* family my mother very big it is for this reason aunts and uncles many I have	My mother's family is very big, so I have many aunts and uncles.

(484) My neighbor is moving out next month. Are you still interested in the apartment?

همسایه‌ی من ماه آینده اسباب‌کشی می‌کند. آیا شما هنوز هم به آپارتمان علاقه دارید؟

hamsaaye_ye man maah_e aayande asbaabkeshi mikonad aayaa shomaa hanuz ham be aapaartemaan 'alaaqe daarid
my neighbor next month moving s/he does I.P. you still too to apartment you are interested

(485) My other daughter is an engineer.

دختر دیگرم مهندس است.

dokhtar_e digaram mohandes ast
daughter my other engineer she is

(486) My parents died many years ago.

پدر و مادرم سال‌ها پیش درگذشتند.

pedar va maadaram saalhaa pish dargozashtand
father and my mother years ago they died

(487) My passport is valid for only two more months, so I should renew it immediately.

گذرنامه‌ی من فقط دو ماه دیگر اعتبار دارد، پس باید فوراً آن را تمدید کنم.

gozarnaame_ye man faqat do maah_e digar e'tebaar daarad, pas baayad foran aan raa tamdid konam
my passport only two month other validity it has so must immediately it D.O. I should renew

(488) My siblings and I have nine children in total.

خواهر و برادران من و خودم، در مجموع نه فرزند داریم.

khaahar va baraadaraan_e man va khodam, dar majmu' noh farzand daarim
sister and my brothers and myself altogether nine child we have

(489) My sister has dark hair, whereas I have blond hair.

خواهرم موهای تیره دارد، در حالی که موهای من بلوند است.

khaaharam muhaa_ye tire daarad, dar haali ke muhaa_ye man belond ast
my sister hair dark she has whereas my hair blond it is

(490) My sister is interested in politics, but I am not interested in it.

خواهرم به سیاست علاقه دارد، اما من به آن علاقه‌ای ندارم.

khaaharam be siyaasat 'alaaqe daarad, ammaa man be aan 'alaaqeiy nadaaram
my sister to politics interest she has but I to that an interest I don't have

(491) My son has grown a lot. He is already taller than me.

پسرم خیلی بزرگ شده است. او از الان، از من بلندتر شده است.

pesaram kheyli bozorg shode ast. u az alaan, az man bolandtar shode ast.

(492) My son is very thin. He eats too little.

پسرم خیلی لاغر است. خیلی کم غذا می‌خورد.

pesaram kheyli laaqar ast. kheyli kam qazaa mikhorad.

(493) My son paints very well. He has a lot of imagination.

پسرم خیلی خوب نقاشی می‌کشد. تخیل خیلی زیادی دارد.

pesaram kheyli khub naqqaashi mikeshad. takhayyol_e kheyli ziyaadi daarad.

(494) My son simply drove away with the car without asking me.

پسرم به سادگی با ماشین رفت، بدون اینکه از من اجازه بگیرد.

pesaram be saadegi baa maashin raft, bedun_e inke az man ejaaze begirad.

(495) My son wants to study medicine and become a doctor like his mother.

پسرم می‌خواهد پزشکی بخواند و مانند مادرش دکتر شود.

pesaram mikhaahad pezeshki bekhaanad va maanand_e maadarash doktor shavad.

(496) My wife is three months pregnant.

همسرم سه ماهه باردار است.

hamsaram se maahe baardaar ast.

(497) My youngest child is four years old.

کوچک‌ترین فرزند من چهار ساله است.

kuchektarin farzand_e man chahaar saal_e ast.

(498) Normally I have to work on Monday, but today is an exception.

معمولاً دوشنبه‌ها باید کار کنم، اما امروز استثناست.

ma'mulan doshanbehaa baayad kaar konam, ammaa emruz estesnaast.

(499) Of course I will help you. You are my friend after all.

البته که به تو کمک می‌کنم. هر چه باشد تو
albatte ke be to komak mikonam. har che baashad to
of course that to you I help whatever it may be you

دوست من هستی.
dust_e man hasti
my friend you are

(500) On Sunday we're having a party. I still have to prepare a lot for it.

روز یکشنبه مهمانی داریم. هنوز خیلی چیزها را باید
ruz_e yekshanbe mehmaani daarim. hanuz kheyli chizhaa raa baayad
day Sunday party we have still many things D.O. must

برای آن آماده کنم.
baraaye aan aamaade konam
for that I should prepare

(501) On the one hand I would like to take the trip, on the other hand it is too expensive.

از یک طرف دوست دارم مسافرت بروم، از طرف
az yek taraf dust daaram mosaaferat beravam, az taraf_e
from one side I like travel I would go from side

دیگر مسافرت خیلی گران است.
digar mosaaferat kheyli geraan ast
other travel very expensive it is

(502) On the second day we took a tour through the harbor.

در روز دوم در بندرگاه گردش کردیم.
dar ruz_e dovvom dar bandargaah gardesh kardim
on day second at harbor we walked around

(503) One can no longer imagine a world without internet.

دیگر کسی نمی‌تواند دنیای بدون اینترنت را
digar kasi nemitavaanad donyaa_ye bedun_e internet raa
anymore somebody s/he can't world without internet D.O.

تصور کند.
tasavvor konad
s/he cannot imagine

(504) One has an amazing view of the city from this tower.

از بالای این برج می‌توان منظره‌ی شگفت‌انگیزی از
az baalaa_ye in borj mitavaan manzare_ye shegeftangizi az
from top this tower may view amazing of

شهر دید.
shahr did
city s/he saw

(505) **Originally, I wanted to be a doctor, but instead I became a dentist.**
اول می‌خواستم دکتر شوم، اما در عوض دندانپزشک شدم.
avval mikhaastam doktor shavam, ammaa dar avaz dandaanpezeshk shodam.

(506) **Our business is going well. Our revenues were higher this month than last.**
کسب و کار ما خوب پیش می‌رود. درآمد ما در این ماه، نسبت به ماه گذشته بالاتر بود.
kasb o kaar_e maa khub pish miravad. daraamad_e maa dar in maah, nesbat be maah_e gozashte baalaatar bud.

(507) **Our company has only seven employees.**
شرکت ما فقط هفت کارمند دارد.
sherkat_e maa faqat haft kaarmand daarad.

(508) **Our dog's hair is all over the house.**
موی سگ ما در تمام خانه ریخته است.
mu_ye sag_e maa dar tamaam_e khaane rikhte ast.

(509) **Our friend's child has been disabled since the accident.**
فرزند دوست ما، از زمان حادثه معلول شده است.
farzand_e dust_e maa, az zamaan_e haadese ma'lul shode ast.

(510) **Our neighbor is very polite. He always says good morning.**
همسایه‌ی ما بسیار مؤدب است. او همیشه صبح بخیر می‌گوید.
hamsaaye_ye maa besyaar mo'addab ast. u hamishe sobh bekheyr miguyad.

(511) **Our rent is very high, but the location is good.**
اجاره‌ی ما خیلی زیاد است، اما موقعیت خانه خوب است.
ejaare_ye maa kheyli ziyaad ast, ammaa moqe'iyyat_e khaane khub ast.

(512) **Our two children are very different from each other.**
دو فرزند ما خیلی با هم تفاوت دارند.
do farzand_e maa kheyli baa ham tafaavot daarand.

(513) Our windows are not airtight. There is always a draft.

پنجره‌های ما عایق هوا نیستند. همیشه در
panjarehaa_ye maa aayeq_e havaa nistand. hamishe dar
our windows insulation air they are not always at

جریان است.
jaryaan ast
flow it is

(514) Pardon me? What did you say?

ببخشید؟ چه گفتید؟
bebakhshid che goftid
pardon what you said

(515) Paris is the capital of France.

پاریس پایتخت فرانسه است.
paaris paaytakht_e faraanse ast
Paris capital France it is

(516) Parliament has enacted a new law.

مجلس یک قانون جدید تصویب کرده است.
majles yek qaanun_e jadid tasvib karde ast
parliament a law new it has approved

(517) People in every country grumble about the weather.

مردم همه‌ی کشورها، از آب و هوا گلایه می‌کنند.
mardom_e hame_ye keshvarhaa az aab o havaa gelaaye mikonand
people all of countries weather they complain

(518) Picasso is perhaps the most famous painter in the world.

پیکاسو احتمالاً مشهورترین نقاش جهان است.
pikaaso ehtemaalan mashhurtarin naqqaash_e jahaan ast
Picasso probably most famous painter world he is

(519) Pick up your clothes off the floor.

لباس‌هایت را از روی زمین بردار!
lebaashaayat raa az ru_ye zamin bardaar
your clothes D.O. from over ground pick up

(520) Please bring me a cup of hot chocolate.

لطفاً یک فنجان شکلات داغ برایم بیاور.
lotfan yek fenjaan shokolaat_e daaq baraayam biyaavar
please a cup chocolate hot for me bring

(521) Please do not throw recycling in the normal garbage.

لطفاً بازیافتی‌ها را در سطل‌های زباله‌ی معمولی
lotfan baazyaaftihaa raa dar satlhaa_ye zobaale_ye ma'muli
please recyclables D.O. in containers trash normal

نیندازید.
nayandaazid
don't throw

(522) Please don't disturb me now. I have to concentrate on my work.

لطفاً الان مزاحم من نشوید. باید بر روی کارم
lotfan alaan mozaahem_e man nashavid. baayad bar ru_ye kaaram
please now troublesome I don't become must on my work

تمرکز کنم.
tamarkoz konam
I should focus

(523) Please get to the airport at least one hour before takeoff.

لطفاً حداقل یک ساعت قبل از پرواز، در فرودگاه باشید.
lotfan haddeaqal yek saa'at qabl az parvaaz dar forudgaah baashid
please at least an hour before flight at airport be

(524) Please justify your opinion.

لطفاً نظر خود را توجیه کنید.
lotfan nazar_e khod raa tojih konid
please opinion self D.O. justify

(525) Please knock before entering.

لطفاً قبل از وارد شدن، در بزنید.
lotfan qabl az vaared shodan dar bezanid
please before entering door hit

(526) Please read this information carefully.

لطفاً این اطلاعات را با دقت بخوانید.
lotfan in ettelaa'aat raa baa deqqat bekhaanid
please this information D.O. with precision read

(527) Please remain seated during takeoff.

لطفاً در طی مدت برخاستن، در حالت نشسته بمانید.
lotfan dar tey_ye moddat_e barkhaastan dar haalat_e neshaste bemaanid
please during time at takeoff condition seated stay

(528) Please remember to turn off the heating before you go to sleep.

لطفاً قبل از خوابیدن، خاموش کردن سیستم گرمایشی را
lotfan qabl az khaabidan khaamush kardan_e sistem_e garmaayeshi raa
please before sleeping turning off system heating D.O.

فراموش نکن!
faraamush nakon
don't forget

(529) Please set your phone to vibrate or silent.

لطفاً گوشیتان را روی حالت بی‌صدا یا لرزش بگذارید.
lotfan gushiyetaan raa ru_ye haalat_e bisedaa yaa larzesh begozaarid
please your phone D.O. over mode silent or vibration put

(530) Please wash your hands before holding the baby.

لطفاً قبل از بغل کردن بچه، دست‌های خود را بشویید.
lotfan qabl az baqal kardan_e bachche dasthaa_ye khod raa beshuiyd
please before hugging baby hands self D.O. wash

(531) Potatoes can be cooked many different ways.

سیب‌زمینی را به روش‌های مختلفی می‌توان پخت.
sibzamini raa be raveshhaa_ye mokhtalefi mitavaan pokht
potato D.O. in methods different it can be cooked

(532) Put the milk in the fridge. Don't leave it on the counter.

شیر را در یخچال بگذارید. آن را روی پیشخوان نگذارید.
shir raa dar yakhchaal begozaarid. aan raa ru_ye pishkhaan nagozaarid.
milk D.O. in refrigerator put. it D.O. on counter don't put.

(533) Read the contract before signing.

قبل از امضای قرارداد، آن را بخوانید.
qabl az emzaa_ye qaraardaad, aan raa bekhaanid.
before signing contract, it D.O. read.

(534) Read the instructions before assembling the table.

قبل از سر هم کردن میز، دستورالعمل را بخوانید.
qabl az sar ham kardan_e miz, dasturol'amal raa bekhaanid.
before assembling table, instruction D.O. read.

(535) Recently the economy has picked up again.

اخیراً اقتصاد دوباره رونق گرفته است.
akhiran eqtesaad dobaare ronaq gerefte ast
recently economy again it has flourished

(536) Religion is very important to some people.

مذهب برای برخی از افراد خیلی مهم است.
mazhab baraaye barkhi az afraad kheyli mohemm ast
religion for some of people very important it is

(537) Rents are very high in this area.

اجاره‌ها در این منطقه خیلی بالاست.
ejaarehaa dar in mantaqe kheyli baalaast.
rents in this area very it's high

(538) Round-trip? No, just one-way please.

سفر رفت و برگشت؟ نه، فقط یک طرفه، لطفاً.
safar_e raft o bargasht? na faqat yek tarafe, lotfan
trip going and returning? no only one way, please

(539) Sara filled her bucket with sand using a plastic shovel.

سارا با استفاده از یک بیل پلاستیکی، سطل خود را از شن پر کرد.
saaraa baa estefaade az yek bil_e pelaastiki, satl_e khod raa az shen por kard.
Sara with using from a shovel plastic, bucket self D.O. from sand she filled

(540) Sara indeed wants to study, but on the other hand, she wants to earn money right away.

سارا واقعاً می‌خواهد تحصیل کند، اما از طرف دیگر، او می‌خواهد فوراً پول در بیاورد.
saaraa vaaqe'an mikhaahad tahsil konad, ammaa az taraf_e digar, u mikhaahad foran pul dar biyaavarad.
Sara really she wants she would study but from side other she she wants immediately she would make money

(541) Scientists are trying to find a cure for cancer.

دانشمندان در حال تلاش برای یافتن درمانی برای سرطان هستند.
daaneshmandaan dar haal_e talaash baraaye yaaftan_e darmaani baraaye sarataan hastand.
scientists ←are trying for finding a cure for cancer they are→

(542) Shall we go grocery shopping and cook together afterwards? - Yes, that sounds good.

بهتر نیست که مواد غذایی را بخریم و بعد از آن، با هم آشپزی کنیم؟ - بله، فکر خوبیست.
behtar nist ke mavaadd_e qazaaiy raa bekharim va ba'd az aan, baa ham aashpazi konim? bale, fekr_e khubist.
better it is not that ingredients food D.O. we would buy and after that together we would cook yes thought it is good

(543) Shall we go to the zoo with the kids on Saturday?

آیا شنبه با بچه‌ها به باغ وحش می‌رویم؟
aayaa shanbe baa bachchehaa be baaq_e vahsh miravim?
I.P. Saturday with kids to zoo we go

(544) She goes for a swim almost every day in the indoor swimming pool.

او تقریباً هر روز در استخر سر پوشیده شنا می‌کند.
u taqriban har ruz dar estakhr_e sar pushide shenaa mikonad.
she almost every day at pool covered she swims

(545) She has been my customer for a long time. I gave her a special price.

او مدت‌هاست که مشتری من است. قیمت ویژه‌ای به او دادم.
u moddathaast ke moshtari_ye man ast. qeymat_e vizheiy be u daadam.
she it is long time that my customer she is price special to she I gave

(546) She has two children from her first marriage.

او از ازدواج اول خود دو فرزند دارد.
u az ezdevaaj_e avval_e khod do farzand daarad.
she from marriage first self two child she has

(547) She heard a strange noise in the attic.

او صدای عجیبی را از اتاق زیر شیروانی شنید.
u sedaa_ye 'ajibi raa az otaaq_e zir_e shirvaani shenid.
she sound strange D.O. from room under pitched roof she heard

(548) She looked out the window of the train as it passed through the countryside.

وقتی قطار از حومه‌ی شهر رد می‌شد، او از پنجره به بیرون نگاه کرد.

vaqti qataar az hume_ye shahr rad mishod, u az panjere be birun negaah kard.
when from train from around city it was passing she from window to outside she looked

(549) She talked a lot, but her husband didn't say a word all evening.

او خیلی صحبت کرد، اما همسرش در تمام طول عصر، یک کلمه هم نگفت.

u kheyli sohbat kard, ammaa hamsarash dar tamaam_e tul_e 'asr, yek kaleme ham nagoft.
she very she talked but her husband at all long evening a word too he did not say

(550) She told me her name, but I forgot it.

او اسمش را به من گفت، اما فراموش کردم.

u esmash raa be man goft, ammaa faraamush kardam.
she her name D.O. to I she said but I forgot

(551) She works for some company in Italy, but I can't remember the name.

او برای شرکتی در ایتالیا کار می‌کند، اما اسمش را یادم نمی‌آید.

u baraaye sherkati dar itaaliyaa kaar mikonad, ammaa esmash raa yaadam nemiaayad.
she for company at Italy she works but its name D.O. my memory it doesn't come

(552) Should we take a taxi or just walk?

تاکسی بگیریم یا همین طور پیاده برویم؟

taaksi begirim yaa hamin tor piyaade beravim?
taxi we would take or this way we would walk

(553) Smoking is prohibited in most restaurants.

در اکثر رستوران‌ها سیگار کشیدن ممنوع است.

dar aksar_e resturaanhaa sigaar keshidan mamnu' ast.
at most restaurants cigarette smoking prohibited it is

(554) So long as you have a fever, you must stay in bed.

تا زمانی که تب دارید، باید در تختخواب بمانید.

taa zamaani ke tab daarid, baayad dar takhtekhaab bemaanid.
until time that fever you have must in bed you should stay

(555) Social media, such as Facebook and Twitter, is addictive.

رسانه‌های اجتماعی، از جمله فیسبوک و توییتر اعتیادآور هستند.

resaanehaa_ye ejtemaa'iy, az jomle feysbuk va tuiter e'tiyaadaavar hastand.
mediums social including Facebook and Twitter addictive they are

(556) Solar panels convert sunlight into electricity.

صفحه‌های خورشیدی، نور خورشید را به برق تبدیل می‌کنند.

safhehaa_ye khorshidi, nur_e khorshid raa be barq tabdil mikonand.
panels solar, light sun D.O. to electricity they convert

(557) Some of the neighbors are unfriendly, but most are nice.

برخی از همسایه‌ها مهربان نیستند، اما بیشتر آنها خوب هستند.

barkhi az hamsaayehaa mehrabaan nistand, ammaa bishtar_e aanhaa khub hastand.
some of neighbors kind they are not, but most they good they are

(558) Sometimes renting is better than buying a house.

گاهی اوقات اجاره کردن خانه بهتر از خریدن آن است.

gaahi oqaat ejaare kardan_e khaane behtar az kharidan_e aan ast.
sometimes renting house better from buying it it is

(559) Sports are ninety percent physical and fifty percent mental.

ورزش‌ها، نود درصد جسمی و پنجاه درصد ذهنی هستند.

varzeshhaa, navad darsad jesmi va panjaah darsad zehni hastand.
sports, ninety percent physical and fifty percent mental they are

(560) Take a few sandwiches with you for the trip.

چند ساندویچ با خودت برای مسافرت ببر.

chand saandevich baa khodat baraaye mosaaferat bebar.
several sandwich with yourself for trip take

(561) Take your time. There's no rush.

عجله نکن. نیازی به عجله نیست.

'ajale nakon. niyaazi be 'ajale nist.
hurry don't do. need to hurry it is not

(562) Talent is futile unless you work hard.

استعداد بی‌فایده است، مگر اینکه سخت کار کنید.

este'daad bifaayde ast, magar inke sakht kaar konid.
talent useless it is, unless hard you would work

(563) Tehran has over eight million residents.

تهران بیش از هشت میلیون نفر جمعیت دارد.

tehraan bish az hasht melyun nafar jam'iyyat daarad.
Tehran more than eight million person population it has

(564) **Tell me all about your trip to Japan.**

همه چیز را دربارهٔ سفر خود به ژاپن به من بگویید.

beguiyd man be zhaapon be khod safar_e darbaare_ye raa hame chiz
tell I to Japan to self trip about D.O. everything

(565) **Tell me the truth. Have you started smoking again?**

حقیقت را به من بگو! آیا دوباره سیگار کشیدن را

raa keshidan sigaar dobaare aayaa begu man be raa haqiqat
D.O. smoking cigarette again I.P. say I to D.O. truth

شروع کرده‌ای؟

shoru' kardeiy
you have started

(566) **Ten percent of the population was born abroad.**

ده درصد از جمعیت، در خارج از کشور متولد شده‌اند.

motevalled shodeand keshvar az khaarej dar jam'iyyat az darsad dah
they were born country of outside at population of percent ten

(567) **Thankfully it didn't rain on our wedding day.**

خوشبختانه در روز عروسی ما باران نیامد.

nayaamad baaraan 'arusi_ye maa ruz_e dar khoshbakhtaane
it didn't come rain our wedding day at fortunately

(568) **That guy is strong. He lifts heavy weights and eats a lot.**

آن مرد قوی است. او وزنه‌های سنگین را بلند می‌کند

boland mikonad raa sangin vaznehaa_ye u ast qavi mard aan
he lifts D.O. heavy weights he he is strong man that

و زیاد می‌خورد.

mikhorad ziyaad va
he eats much and

(569) **That is Alex. He lives next door.**

این الکس است. او در خانه‌ی کناری ما

maa kenaari_ye khaane_ye dar u ast aleks in
we next house at he he is Alex this

زندگی می‌کند.

zendegi mikonad
he lives

(570) **That is totally out of the question!**

این مسئله اصلاً قابل بحث نیست!

nist qaabel_e bahs aslan mas'ale in
it is not arguable at all problem this

(571) **That store is open six days per week.**

آن فروشگاه شش روز در هفته باز است.

ast baaz hafte dar ruz shesh forushgaah aan
it is open week at day six store that

(572) That was a terribly awkward interaction. I'm glad it's over.

آن ارتباط بسیار ناخوشایند بود. خوشحالم که تمام شد.
aan ertebaat besyaar naakhoshaayand bud. khoshhaalam ke taamam shod.
that communication very awkward it was I'm happy that it was finished

(573) That was an embarrassing situation.

آن وضعیت شرم‌آور بود.
aan vaz'iyyat sharmaavar bud.
that situation embarrassing it was

(574) That's a crazy story. Did it really happen?

این یک داستان مسخره است. آیا واقعاً اتفاق افتاده است؟
in yek daastaan_e maskhare ast. aayaa vaaqe'an ettefaaq oftaade ast?
this a story ridiculous it is I.P. really it has happened

(575) The airport is located outside of the city.

این فرودگاه در خارج از شهر واقع شده است.
in forudgaah dar khaarej az shahr vaaqe' shode ast.
this airport at outside of city it is located

(576) The ambulance took my mom to the hospital.

آمبولانس مادرم را به بیمارستان برد.
aambulaans maadaram raa be bimaarestaan bord.
ambulance my mother D.O. to hospital it took

(577) The apartment has one main drawback. It is not centrally located.

آپارتمان یک اشکال اصلی دارد. موقعیت مرکزی ندارد.
aapaartemaan yek eshkaal_e asli daarad. moqe'iyyat_e markazi nadaarad.
apartment a problem main it has location central it doesn't have

(578) The baby has such little fingers and toes!

انگشتان دست و پای این بچه خیلی کوچک است.
angoshtaan_e dast o paa_ye in bachche kheyli kuchak ast.
fingers hand and foot this baby very little it is

(579) The bill is due at the end of the month.

سر رسید قبض در پایان ماه است.
sar resid_e qabz dar paayaan_e maah ast.
due date bill at end month it is

(580) The bill is wrong. The waiter made a mistake.

این صورتحساب اشتباه است. پیشخدمت اشتباه کرده است.
in surathesaab eshtebaah ast. pishkhedmat eshtebaah karde ast
this bill wrong it is. waiter s/he has made a mistake

(581) The bird flew to its nest.

پرنده به سمت لانه‌ی خود پرواز کرد.
parande be samt_e laane_ye khod parvaaz kard
bird to direction nest self it flew

(582) The book will be published this year.

این کتاب امسال منتشر می‌شود.
in ketaab emsaal montasher mishavad
this book this year it is published

(583) The book you're looking for is on the top shelf.

کتابی که دنبالش هستید، بر روی قفسه بالایی است.
ketaabi ke donbaalash hastid, bar ru_ye qafase_ye baalaaiy ast
book that its looking you are on shelf top it is

(584) The boss isn't around right now. He is normally in the office at this time.

رییس در حال حاضر این اطراف نیست. این موقع او معمولاً در اداره است.
raiys dar haal_e haazer in atraaf nist. in moqe' u ma'mulan dar edaare ast
boss currently this around he is not. this time he usually in office he is

(585) The bread is fresh and smells wonderful.

نان تازه است و بوی فوق‌العاده‌ای می‌دهد.
naan taaze ast va bu_ye foqolaaddeiy midahad
bread fresh it is and smell wonderful it gives

(586) The car is now fifteen years old, but it still runs well.

این اتومبیل اکنون پانزده سال دارد، اما هنوز هم خوب کار می‌کند.
in otomobil aknun paanzdah saal daarad, ammaa hanuz ham khub kaar mikonad
this car now fifteen year it has, but still too good it works

(587) The car needs new tires.

ماشین لاستیک‌های جدیدی لازم دارد.
maashin laastikhaa_ye jadidi laazem daarad
car tires new need it has

English	Farsi (transliteration / gloss)	#
The cash register is at the front. You have to get in line.	صندوق پول در جلو است. شما باید در صف بایستید. sandoq_e pul dar jelo ast. shomaa baayad dar saf beiystid. cash register at front it is. you must in line you should stand	(588)
The celebration is a good opportunity to see our friends.	این جشن فرصت خوبی برای دیدن دوستانمان است. in jashn forsat_e khubi baraaye didan_e dustaanemaan ast. this celebration opportunity good for seeing our friends it is	(589)
The chair is made of plastic, not wood.	صندلی از جنس پلاستیک است نه چوب. sandali az jens_e pelaastik ast na chub. chair from material plastic it is not wood	(590)
The child takes a short nap every day after lunch.	کودک هر روز بعد از ناهار چرت کوتاهی می‌زند. kudak har ruz ba'd az naahaar chort_e kutaahi mizanad. child every day after lunch short s/he takes a nap	(591)
The children behaved very well today.	بچه‌ها امروز خیلی خوب رفتار کردند. bachchehaa emruz kheyli khub raftaar kardand. children today very good they behaved	(592)
The city is paying for half of the costs of the project.	این شهر نیمی از هزینه‌های پروژه را پرداخت می‌کند. in shahr nimi az hazinehaa_ye perozhe raa pardaakht mikonad. this city half of costs project D.O. it pays	(593)
The closest emergency room is just one street over.	نزدیک‌ترین اورژانس فقط یک خیابان آن طرف‌تر است. nazdiktarin urzhaans faqat yek khiyaabaan aan taraftar ast. nearest emergency only a street over it is	(594)
The coat won't fit in the suitcase.	کت در چمدان جای نمی‌گیرد. kot dar chamedaan jaay nemigirad. coat in suitcase it doesn't fit	(595)
The coffee is very strong.	این قهوه خیلی غلیظ است. in qahve kheyli qaliz ast. this coffee very strong it is	(596)
The coffee machine is quite easy to operate.	کار کردن با دستگاه قهوه‌ساز خیلی آسان است. kaar kardan baa dastgaah_e qahvesaaz kheyli aasaan ast. working with machine coffee maker very easy it is	(597)

(598)	ارتباط میان بخش‌ها خوب است. ertebaat_e miyaan_e bakhshhaa khub ast communication between departments good it is	The communication between the departments is good.
(599)	شرکت محصول جدیدی را توسعه داده است. sherkat mahsul_e jadidi raa tose'e daade ast company product new D.O. it has developed	The company developed a new product.
(600)	شرکت بسیاری از کارمندان را از کار بیکار کرد. sherkat besyaari az kaarmandaan raa az kaar bikaar kard company many of employees D.O. from work unemployed it did	The company laid off many employees.
(601)	این شرکت به کارکنانش فرصت حضور در دوره‌های زبان را داد. in sherkat be kaarkonaanash forsat_e hozur dar dowrehaa_ye zabaan raa daad this company to its employees opportunity attendance at courses language D.O. it gave	The company offers its employees the chance to attend language courses.
(602)	شرکت هزینه‌های سفرم را به من بر می‌گرداند. sherkat hazinehaa_ye safaram raa be man bar migardaanad company costs my travel D.O. to I it returns	The company pays me back for my travel costs.
(603)	شرکت امسال سه نفر جدید استخدام می‌کند. sherkat emsaal se nafar_e jadid estekhdaam mikonad company this year three person new it employs	The company will hire three new people this year.
(604)	مهلت ثبت‌نام این دوره تمام شده است. mohlat_e sabt_e naam_e in dowre tamaam shode ast deadline registering this course it has been finished	The deadline for registering for this course has passed.
(605)	تا پس فردا امکان نوبت‌دهی برای دندانپزشک وجود ندارد. taa pas fardaa emkaan_e nobatdehi baraaye dandaanpezeshk vojud nadaarad until after tomorrow possibility turn-giving for dentist there is not	The dentist appointment is not until the day after tomorrow.
(606)	پزشک معاینه‌ام کرد، اما نتوانست مشکلی پیدا کند. pezeshk mo'aayneam kard ammaa natavaanest moshkeli peydaa konad doctor my examination s/he did but s/he could not a problem s/he could find	The doctor examined me but couldn't find anything wrong.

(607) دکتر مرا سرزنش کرد، چون واقعاً دارم چاق می‌شوم.

The doctor laid into me because I'm getting really fat.

mishavam chaaq daaram vaaqe'an chon sarzanesh kard maraa doktor
I become→ fat ←I am really because s/he reproached me doctor

(608) دکتر می‌گوید من باید ورزش کنم، مثلاً شنا یا دوچرخه‌سواری کنم.

The doctor says I have to exercise, for example, swimming or riding a bicycle.

yaa shenaa masalan varzesh konam baayad man miguyad doktor
or swimming for example I should exercise must I s/he says doctor

konam docharkhesavaari
I would do bicycle-riding

(609) در به طور خودکار بسته می‌شود.

The door closes automatically.

baste mishavad khodkaar tor_e be dar
it is closed automatic way to door

(610) اقتصاد دچار یک بحران جدی است.

The economy is in a serious crisis.

ast jeddi bohraan_e yek dochaar_e eqtesaad
it is serious crisis a stricken economy

(611) آسانسور خراب است.

The elevator is out of order.

ast kharaab aasaansor
it is broken elevator

(612) خروجی اضطراری، درست اینجا کنار پله‌هاست.

The emergency exit is right here by the stairs.

pellehaast kenaar_e injaa dorost ezteraari khoruji_ye
(it is) stairs by here right emergency exit

(613) کارخانه رودخانه را آلوده می‌کند.

The factory pollutes the river.

aalude mikonad raa rudkhaane kaarkhaane
it pollutes D.O. river factory

(614) آتش بسیاری از خانه‌ها را ویران کرد.

The fire destroyed many houses.

viraan kard raa khaanehaa az besyaari aatash
it destroyed D.O. houses from many fire

(615) آتش به سرعت خاموش شد.

The fire was quickly extinguished.

shod khaamush be sor'at aatash
it became extinguished quickly fire

(616) پرواز کوتاه بود. کمتر از یک ساعت.

The flight was short. Just under an hour.

saa'at yek az kamtar bud kutaah parvaaz
hour an than less it was short flight

(617)	گل‌ها باز شده‌اند. بهار است. *ast bahaar shodeand baaz golhaa* it is spring they have become open flowers	The flowers are already blooming. It's spring.
(618)	غذا و امکانات اقامتی عالی بود. *bud 'aali eqaamati emkaanaat_e va qazaa* it was excellent accommodation facilities and food	The food and accommodation were excellent.
(619)	غذا برای من خیلی شور است. *ast shur kheyli man baraaye qazaa* it is salty very I for food	The food is too salty for me.
(620)	دانشجویان خارجی ابتدا باید در یک دوره‌ی زبان شرکت کنند. *zabaan dowre_ye yek dar baayad ebtedaa khaareji daaneshjuyaan_e* language course a at must first foreign students *sherkat konand* they should participate	The foreign students must first attend a language course.
(621)	سطل زباله پر است. *ast por zobaale satl_e* it is full trash bin	The garbage can is full.
(622)	سطل‌های زباله پیاده‌رو را بسته‌اند. *basteand raa piyaadero zobaale satlhaa_ye* they have closed D.O. sidewalk trash bins	The garbage cans are blocking the sidewalk.
(623)	امشب باید زباله‌ها بیرون برده شوند. *borde shavand birun zobaalehaa baayad emshab* they should be taken outside trash must tonight	The garbage must be taken out tonight.
(624)	ترجمه‌ی آلمانی آن کتاب تقریباً به خوبی زبان اصلی آن بود. *zabaan_e be khubi_ye taqriban ketaab aan aalmaani_ye tarjome_ye* language as good as almost book that German translation *bud aan asli_ye* it was it original	The German translation of that book is nearly as good as the original.
(625)	لیوان به زمین افتاد و شکست. *shekast va oftaad zamin be livaan* it broke and it fell ground to glass	The glass fell to the floor and broke.
(626)	دولت باید به حرف مردم گوش کند. *gush konad mardom harf_e be baayad dolat* it should listen people speech (of) to must government	The government should listen to the people.

(627) **The government will surely raise taxes soon.**
دولت مطمئناً به زودی مالیات را افزایش خواهد داد.
dolat motma'ennan be zudi maaliyaat raa afzaayesh khaahad daad
government surely soon taxes D.O. it will increase

(628) **The heart is a symbol of love.**
قلب نماد عشق است.
qalb namaad_e eshq ast
heart symbol love it is

(629) **The hotel bed was too soft for me.**
تختخواب هتل برای من بیش از حد نرم بود.
takhtekhaab_e hotel baraaye man bish az hadd narm bud
bed hotel for I too soft it was

(630) **The hotel is located about 10 meters from the beach.**
هتل در حدود ده متری ساحل قرار دارد.
hotel dar hodud_e dah metri_ye saahel qaraar daarad
hotel at around ten meter beach it is located

(631) **The house looks like it was built two hundred years ago.**
به نظر می‌رسد این خانه، دویست سال پیش ساخته شده است.
be nazar miresad in khaane, devist saal_e pish saakhte shode ast
it seems this house two hundred year ago it has been built

(632) **The instructions say that the oldest takes the first turn in this game.**
دستورالعمل می‌گوید که مسن‌ترین فرد بازی را شروع می‌کند.
dasturol'amal miguyad ke mosentarin fard baazi raa shoru' mikonad
instruction it says that oldest person game D.O. s/he starts

(633) **The internet makes my work much easier.**
اینترنت کار من را بسیار آسان‌تر می‌کند.
internet kaar_e man raa besyaar aasaantar mikonad
internet my work D.O. much easier it does

(634) **The invention of printing was very important for mankind.**
اختراع چاپ برای بشر بسیار مهم بود.
ekhteraa'_e chaap baraaye bashar besyaar mohemm bud
invention printing for mankind very important it was

(635) **The jacket is missing a button.**
یک دکمه این ژاکت افتاده است.
yek dokme_ye in zhaakat oftaade ast
a button this jacket it has fallen

(636) The jacket is too tight on me.
این ژاکت برای من خیلی تنگ است.
in zhaakat baraaye man kheyli tang ast
this jacket for I very tight it is

(637) The kids laughed at the silly joke.
بچه‌ها به شوخی احمقانه خندیدند.
bachchehaa be shukhi_ye ahmaqaane khandidand
kids at joke silly they laughed

(638) The knife doesn't cut well. You should sharpen it.
چاقو به خوبی نمی‌برد. شما باید آن را تیز کنید.
chaaqu be khubi nemiborad. shomaa baayad aan raa
knife well it doesn't cut you must that D.O.
tiz konid
you should sharpen

(639) The landscape there is very hilly.
چشم انداز آنجا پر از تپه است.
cheshm andaaz_e aanjaa por az tappe ast
landscape there full of hill it is

(640) The laundry is still damp.
لباس‌های شسته شده هنوز مرطوب است.
lebaashaa_ye shoste shode hanuz martub ast
clothes washed still damp it is

(641) The leaves are already changing colors.
برگ‌ها از الان شروع به تغییر رنگ کرده‌اند.
barghaa az alaan shoru' be taqiyr_e rang kardeand
leaves from now begin to change color they have done

(642) The lemonade is too sweet. You added too much sugar.
لیموناد بیش از حد شیرین است. خیلی شکر اضافه کرده‌ای.
limunaad bish az hadd shirin ast kheyli shekar
lemonade too sweet it is much sugar
ezaafe kardeiy
you have added

(643) The longer I learn Arabic, the better I can understand it.
هر چه بیشتر زبان عربی یاد بگیرم، بهتر می‌توانم آن را درک کنم.
har che bishtar zabaan_e 'arabi yaad begiram behtar mitavaanam aan
the more language Arabic I would learn better I can that
raa dark konam
D.O. I would understand

(644) The majority of people in the world own a cell phone.
اکثر مردم دنیا، تلفن همراه دارند.
aksar_e mardom_e donyaa telefon_e hamraah daarand
most people world cell phone they have

(645) The milk is in the fridge on the bottom shelf.

شیر در طبقه‌ی پایین یخچال قرار دارد.

qaraar daarad yakhchaal paaiyn_e tabaqe_ye dar shir
it is located refrigerator bottom shelf at milk

(646) The mirror isn't hanging straight.

آینه صاف آویزان نشده است.

aavizaan nashode ast saaf aayne
it hasn't been hanged straight mirror

(647) The mountain is almost 3000 m high.

ارتفاع این کوه تقریباً سه هزار متر است.

ast metr hezaar se taqriban kuh in ertefaa'_e
it is meter thousand three almost mountain this height

(648) The movie star has long, blond hair.

موی این ستاره فیلم بلند و بور است.

ast bur va boland film setaare_ye in mu_ye
it is blond and long movie star this hair

(649) The movie was great. The actors were very good.

این فیلم عالی بود. بازیگران خیلی خوب بودند.

budand khub kheyli baazigaraan bud 'aali film in
they were good very actors it was great movie this

(650) The movie was very boring and predictable.

این فیلم خیلی کسل کننده و قابل پیش‌بینی بود.

bud qaabel_e pish bini va kesel konande kheyli film in
it was predictable and boring very movie this

(651) The movie was very funny. We laughed a lot.

فیلم خیلی خنده‌دار بود. ما خیلی خندیدیم.

khandidim kheyli maa bud khandedaar kheyli film
we laughed a lot we it was funny very movie

(652) The music is getting on my nerves.

این موسیقی روی اعصاب من است.

ast a'saab_e man ru_ye musiqi in
it is my nerves on music this

(653) The next tour begins in 15 minutes.

گشت بعدی پانزده دقیقه‌ی بعد شروع می‌شود.

shoru' mishavad ba'd daqiqe_ye paanzdah ba'di gasht_e
it is begun next minute fifteen next tour

(654) The number of participants is limited to 12.

تعداد شرکت‌کنندگان به دوازده نفر محدود شده است.

mahdud shode ast nafar davaazdah be sherkat konandegaan te'daad_e
it has been limited person twelve to participants number

(655) The only animal I eat is fish.

تنها حیوانی که می‌خورم ماهی است.

ast maahi mikhoram ke heyvaani tanhaa
it is fish I eat that animal only

(656) The operation went well. We can discharge you tomorrow from the hospital.

عمل به خوبی پیش رفت. می‌توانیم شما را فردا از بیمارستان مرخص کنیم.

'amal (operation) *be khubi* (well) *pish raft* (it progressed) *mitavaanim* (we can) *shomaa raa* (you) *fardaa* (tomorrow) *az* (from) *bimaarestaan* (hospital) *morakhkhas konim* (we can discharge)

(657) The opposite of "small" is "big".

متضاد «کوچک»، «بزرگ» است.

motezaadd_e (opposite) *kuchak* (small) *bozorg* (big) *ast* (it is)

(658) The original is for you. We keep the copy.

نسخه اصلی برای شماست. ما نسخه کپی را نگه می‌داریم.

noskhe_ye (version) *asli* (original) *baraaye shomaast* (it's for you) *maa* (we) *noskhe_ye* (version) *kopi* (copy) *raa* (D.O.) *negah midaarim* (we keep)

(659) The outdoor concert will be canceled if it rains.

در صورت بارش باران، کنسرت در فضای باز لغو می‌شود.

dar surat_e (in case) *baaresh_e* (pouring) *baaraan* (rain) *konsert* (concert) *dar* (at) *fazaa_ye* (space) *baaz* (open) *laqv mishavad* (it is canceled)

(660) The package is ready for pickup at the post office.

بسته در اداره پست آماده فرستادن است.

baste (package) *dar* (at) *edaare_ye* (office) *post* (post) *aamaade_ye* (ready) *ferestaadan* (picking-up) *ast* (it is)

(661) The pants are too long. Can you make them shorter?

این شلوار خیلی بلند است. می‌توانید آن را کوتاه‌تر کنید؟

in (this) *shalvaar* (pants) *kheyli* (very) *boland* (long) *ast* (it is) *mitavaanid* (you can) *aan* (that) *raa* (D.O.) *kutaahtar* (shorter) *konid* (you can make)

(662) The people are a bit different here than in the south.

مردم اینجا کمی متفاوت از مردم جنوب هستند.

mardom_e (people) *injaa* (here) *kami* (a bit) *motefaavet* (different) *az* (from) *mardom_e* (people) *jonub* (south) *hastand* (they are)

(663) The people are fleeing and requesting asylum.

مردم در حال فرار کردن هستند و درخواست پناهندگی دارند.

mardom dar haal_e faraar kardan hastand va darkhaast_e panaahandegi daarand
people at condition escaping they are and request asylum they have

(664) The people are protesting against the coal plant.

مردم نسبت به کارخانه ذغال‌سنگ معترض هستند.

mardom nesbat be kaarkhaane_ye zoqaalsang mo'tarez hastand
people relation to factory coal they are protesting

(665) The police found the weapon.

پلیس اسلحه را پیدا کرد.

polis aslahe raa peydaa kard
police weapon D.O. it found

(666) The police have finally caught the culprit.

سرانجام پلیس مجرم را گرفت.

saranjaam polis mojrem raa gereft
finally police culprit D.O. it caught

(667) The police stopped me because I drove through a red traffic light.

پلیس مرا به دلیل رد کردن چراغ قرمز متوقف کرد.

polis maraa be dalil_e rad kardan_e cheraaq_e qermez motevaqqef kard
police me for reason skipping light red it stopped

(668) The problem is not difficult. The solution is very simple.

این مشکل سخت نیست. راه حلش بسیار ساده است.

in moshkel sakht nist. raah_e hallash besyaar saade ast
this problem difficult it is not. its solution very simple it is

(669) The professor is internationally known.

این پروفسور در سطح بین‌المللی شناخته شده است.

in porofesor dar sath_e beynolmelali shenaakhte shode ast
this professor at level international s/he has been known

(670) The repair is too expensive. I can get it done for half elsewhere.

این دستمزد تعمیر خیلی گران است. می‌توانم آن را با نصف قیمت، جای دیگری انجام دهم.

in dastmozd_e ta'miyr kheyli geraan ast. mitavaanam aan raa baa nesf_e qeymat, jaa_ye digari anjaam daham
this fee repair very expensive it is. I can that D.O. with half price place different I can do

(671) The reporter is currently conducting an interview.

خبرنگار اکنون در حال مصاحبه است.

khabarnegaar aknun dar haal_e mosaahebe ast
journalist now at present interview s/he is

The rice has to cook for about 40 minutes.	برنج باید حدود چهل دقیقه بپزد. *berenj baayad hodud_e chehel daqiqe bepazad* rice must around forty minute it should cook	(672)
The rug is two meters long and one meter wide.	این قالیچه دو متر طول و یک متر عرض دارد. *in qaaliche do metr tul va yek metr 'arz daarad* this rug two meter length and one meter width it has	(673)
The sooner we get there, the better our chances of getting a good seat.	هر چه زودتر به آنجا برسیم، احتمال گیر آوردن *har che zudtar be aanjaa beresim, ehtemaal_e gir aavardan_e* the sooner to there we would arrive possibility getting یک صندلی خوب بیشتر می‌شود. *yek sandali_ye khub bishtar mishavad* a seat good more it becomes	(674)
The stove was still hot. I accidentally burned myself.	اجاق گاز هنوز داغ بود. اتفاقی خودم را سوزاندم. *ojaaq_e gaaz hanuz daaq bud. ettefaaqi khodam raa suzaandam* stove gas still hot it was accidentally myself D.O. I burned	(675)
The student got a good grade for her presentation.	دانش‌آموز برای ارائه‌ی خود، نمره خوبی گرفت. *daaneshaamuz baraaye eraae_ye khod nomre_ye khubi gereft* student for presentation self grade good s/he received	(676)
The students of this school wear standardized uniforms.	دانش‌آموزان این مدرسه لباس استاندارد دارند. *daaneshaamuzaan_e in madrese lebaas_e estaandaard daarand* students this school clothes standard they have	(677)
The suitcase is much too heavy for me to carry.	حمل این چمدان برای من خیلی سنگین است. *haml_e in chamedaan baraaye man kheyli sangin ast* carrying this suitcase for I very heavy it is	(678)
The suitcase is very light. I can carry it alone.	چمدان بسیار سبک است. من می‌توانم به تنهایی آن *chamedaan besyaar sabok ast. man mitavaanam be tanhaaei aan* suitcase very light it is I I can alone it را ببرم. *raa bebaram* D.O. I can take	(679)
This jacket does not fit me anymore.	این ژاکت دیگر اندازه‌ی من نیست. *in zhaakat digar andaaze_ye man nist* this jacket anymore my size it is not	(680)

(681) معلم من را صدا زد تا به این سوال پاسخ دهم.
mo'allem man raa sedaa zad taa be in soaal paasokh daham
teacher me s/he called so to this question I would answer

The teacher called on me to answer the question.

(682) معلم اشتباهات من را تصحیح کرد.
mo'allem eshtebaahaat_e man raa tashih kard
teacher my mistakes D.O. s/he corrected

The teacher corrected my mistakes.

(683) معلم امروز تکلیف درسی زیادی داد.
mo'allem emruz taklif_e darsi_ye ziyaadi daad
teacher today homework a lot s/he gave

The teacher gave a lot of homework today.

(684) معلم دربارهٔ جنگ جهانی دوم صحبت می‌کند.
mo'allem darbaare_ye jang_e jahaani_ye dovvom sohbat mikonad
teacher about war world second s/he speaks

The teacher is lecturing about the Second World War.

(685) معلم گفت ما باید دو فصل این کتاب را دوباره بخوانیم.
mo'allem goft maa baayad do fasl_e in ketaab raa dobaare bekhaanim
teacher s/he said we must two chapter this book D.O. again we should read

The teacher said we should re-read two chapters in the book.

(686) توضیح معلم، بهتر از توضیح داخل کتاب است.
tozih_e mo'allem behtar az tozih_e daakhel_e ketaab ast
explanation teacher better from explanation inside book it is

The teacher's explanation is better than the explanation in the book.

(687) تیم فرانسه حریف خیلی قدرتمندی بود.
tim_e faraanse harif_e kheyli qodratmandi bud
team France opponent very strong it was

The team from France was a very strong opponent.

(688) این تیم در این فصل، فقط یک بازی باخته است.
in tim dar in fasl faqat yek baazi baakhte ast
this team at this season only a game it has lost

The team lost only one game this season.

(689) قوری چای تقریباً خالی است. چای بیشتری برای خودمان درست می‌کنم.
quri_ye chaay taqriban khaali ast. chaay_e bishtari baraaye khodemaan dorost mikonam
pot tea almost empty it is. tea more for ourselves I make

The teapot is almost empty. I'll make us more tea.

83

(690) The temperature has quite suddenly fallen below zero.

دما کاملاً ناگهانی به زیر صفر سقوط کرده است.
damaa kaamelan naagahaani be zir_e sefr soqut karde ast
temperature completely suddenly to below zero it has fallen

(691) The thunder came ten seconds after the lightning.

صدای رعد، ده ثانیه پس از برق آمد.
sedaa_ye ra'd dah saaniye pas az barq aamad
sound thunder ten second after lightning it came

(692) The topic of parenting interests me very much because I am pregnant.

موضوع پرورش فرزند خیلی نظرم را جلب کرده، چون باردار هستم.
mozu'_e parvaresh_e farzand kheyli nazaram raa jalb karde chon baardaar hastam
topic nurture child very my attention D.O. it has attracted because pregnant I am

(693) The tourist visa is valid for ninety days.

ویزای توریستی نود روز اعتبار دارد.
vizaa_ye turisti navad ruz e'tebaar daarad
visa tourist ninety day validity it has

(694) The towels are on the top shelf.

حوله‌ها بر روی قفسه‌ی بالایی هستند.
holehaa bar ru_ye qafase_ye baalaaei hastand
towels on shelf top they are

(695) The traffic light was broken. A policeman directed traffic.

چراغ قرمز خراب بود. مأمور پلیس ترافیک را هدایت می‌کرد.
cheraaq_e qermez kharaab bud ma'mur_e polis teraafik raa hedaayat mikard
light red broken it was officer police traffic D.O. s/he directed

(696) The train comes in 30 minutes. Until then, we can sit here and chat.

قطار سی دقیقه دیگر می‌آید. تا آن زمان می‌توانیم در اینجا بنشینیم و گپ بزنیم.
qataar si daqiqe_ye digar miaayad taa aan zamaan mitavaanim dar injaa beneshinim va gap bezanim
train thirty minute another it comes until that time we can at here we can sit and we can chat

(697) The universe is very large.

کائنات بسیار بزرگ است.
kaaenaat besyaar bozorg ast
universe very large it is

(698) The walls are very thin here. You can hear everything.

دیوارهای اینجا بسیار نازک است. می‌توانید همه چیز را بشنوید.
divaarhaa_ye injaa besyaar naazok ast mitavaanid hame chiz raa beshnavid
walls here very thin it is you can everything D.O. you can hear

(699) The washing machine comes with a one-year warranty.

ماشین لباسشویی یک سال گارانتی دارد.
maashin_e lebaasshuiy yek saal gaaraanti daarad
machine washing a year warranty it has

(700) The wheel was invented about 6000 years ago.

چرخ در حدود شش‌هزار سال پیش اختراع شد.
charkh dar hodud_e shesh hezaar saal_e pish ekhteraa' shod
wheel at about six thousand year ago it was invented

(701) The whole house smells of fresh paint.

کل خانه بوی رنگ تازه می‌دهد.
koll_e khaane bu_ye rang_e taaze midahad
whole house smell paint fresh it gives

(702) The window was not closed during the storm, so a lot of rain came in.

پنجره در هنگام طوفان بسته نبود، بنابراین باران زیادی داخل آمد.
panjere dar hengaam_e tufaan baste nabud banaabarin baaran_e ziyaadi daakhel aamad
window at during storm it was not closed so rain much inside it came

(703) The workers are striking for higher wages.

کارگران برای دستمزد بالاتر اعتصاب می‌کنند.
kaargaraan baraaye dastmozd_e baalaatar e'tesaab mikonand
workers for wage higher they strike

(704) There are 15 boys and 10 girls in the class.

پانزده پسر و ده دختر، در این کلاس هستند.
paanzdah pesar va dah dokhtar dar in kelaas hastand
fifteen boy and ten girl at this class they are

(705) There are big cultural differences between the countries.

تفاوت‌های فرهنگی بزرگی بین کشورها وجود دارد.
tafaavothaa_ye farhangi_ye bozorgi beyn_e keshvarhaa vojud daarad
differences cultural big between countries there is

(706) There are many benefits to learning another language.

یادگیری یک زبان دیگر، مزایای زیادی دارد.
yaadgiri_ye yek zabaan_e digar mazaayaa_ye ziyaadi daarad
learning a language another advantages many it has

There are many famous museums in Paris.	موزه‌های خیلی مشهوری در پاریس هستند. hastand paaris dar mashhuri kheyli muzehaa_ye they are Paris in famous very museums	(707)
There are many hiking trails in this area.	مسیرهای پیاده‌روی زیادی در این منطقه وجود دارد. vojud daarad mantaqe in dar ziyaadi piyaaderavi_ye masirhaa_ye there is area this in many walking paths	(708)
There are many social problems in this country.	مشکلات اجتماعی زیادی در این کشور وجود دارد. vojud daarad keshvar in dar ziyaadi ejtemaa'iy_ye moshkelaat_e there is country this at many social problems	(709)
There are many ways to prepare a chicken.	برای تهیه‌ی مرغ، روش‌های زیادی هست. hast ziyaadi raveshhaa_ye morq tahiyye_ye baraaye it is many ways chicken preparing for	(710)
There are no visible injuries, but we should examine the leg anyway.	آسیب‌دیدگی مشهودی وجود ندارد، اما در هر صورت، dar har surat ammaa vojud nadaarad mashhudi aasibdidegi in any case but there is not visible injury بهتر است پا را معاینه کنیم. mo'aayene konim raa paa ast behtar we should examine D.O. leg it is better	(711)
There are still tickets available for the concert next week.	بلیت کنسرت هفته‌ی آینده هنوز موجود است. ast mojud hanuz aayaande hafte_ye konsert_e belit_e it is available still next week concert ticket	(712)
There are three outlets in this room.	در این اتاق، سه پریز هست. hast piriz se otaaq in dar it is outlet three room this in	(713)
There is a detour because of the accident.	به دلیل تصادف، یک مسیر انحرافی وجود دارد. vojud daarad enheraafi masir_e yek tasaadof dalil_e be there is deviation path a accident reason to	(714)
There is a discount for children and seniors.	تخفیف برای کودکان و سالمندان موجود است. ast mojud saalmandaan va kudakaan baraaye takhfif it is available seniors and children for discount	(715)
There is a great view of the city from here.	اینجا نمای خیلی خوبی از شهر دارد. daarad shahr az khubi kheyli namaa_ye injaa it has city from good very view here	(716)
There is no soap in the restroom.	سرویس بهداشتی صابون ندارد. nadaarad saabun servis_e behdaashti it doesn't have soap restroom/W.C.	(717)

(718)	There is still a bit of wine left. Would you like any more?	هنوز مقدار کمی شراب مانده است. باز هم می‌خواهید؟ *hanuz meqdaar_e kami sharaab maande ast. baaz ham mikhaahid* (still amount little wine it has been left. still you want)
(719)	There was a delicious dessert after the meal.	یک دسر خوشمزه بعد از غذا داشتیم. *yek deser_e khoshmaze ba'd az qazaa daashtim* (a dessert delicious after meal we had)
(720)	These are my friends, so please be nice to them.	اینها دوستان من هستند، پس لطفاً با آنها خوب باشید. *inhaa dustaan_e man hastand, pas lotfan baa aanhaa khub baashid* (these my friends they are so please with they good be)
(721)	These big trucks are used to transport goods over long distances.	این کامیون‌های بزرگ، برای حمل و نقل کالا در مسافت‌های طولانی استفاده می‌شوند. *in kaamiyunhaa_ye bozorg, baraaye haml o naql_e kaalaa dar masaafathaa_ye tulaani estefaade mishavand* (this trucks big for transportation goods at distances long they are used)
(722)	These painkillers are available only by prescription.	این مسکن‌ها فقط با نسخه داده می‌شوند. *in mosakkenhaa faqat baa noskhe daade mishavand* (this painkillers only with prescription they are given)
(723)	They are looking for experts in this computer programming language.	آنها به دنبال متخصصانی در این زبان برنامه‌نویسی کامپیوتری هستند. *aanhaa be donbaal_e motekhassesaani dar in zabaan_e barnaamenevisi_ye kaampiyuteri hastand* (they ←looking for experts at this language program-writing computer they are→)
(724)	They both agreed to my proposal.	هر دوی آنها با پیشنهاد من موافقت کردند. *har do_ye aanhaa baa pishnehaad_e man mowaafeqat kardand* (every two they with my proposal they agreed)
(725)	They couldn't afford to pay for a big wedding.	آنها نمی‌توانستند هزینه‌ی یک عروسی مفصل را بپردازند. *aanhaa nemitavaanestand hazine_ye yek 'arusi_ye mofassal raa bepardaazand* (they they couldn't cost a wedding elaborate D.O. they could pay)

(726) They need more exercise. They should go walking regularly.

آنها به ورزش بیشتری نیاز دارند. باید به طور مرتب پیاده‌روی کنند.

aanhaa be varzesh_e bishtari niyaaz daarand. baayad be tor_e morattab piyaaderavi konand.
they to exercise more need they have. must to way regular they should walk.

(727) This airplane flies directly to New York.

این هواپیما مستقیم به نیویورک پرواز می‌کند.

in havaapeymaa mostaqim be niyoyork parvaaz mikonad.
this airplane direct to New York it flies.

(728) This car is the safest in its class.

این ماشین در رده خودش ایمن‌ترین است.

in maashin dar rade khodash imentarin ast.
this car in class itself safest it is.

(729) This coat costs more than that one, but it's worth it.

قیمت این کت بیشتر از آن یکی است، اما ارزشش را دارد.

qeymat_e in kot bishtar az aan yeki ast, ammaa arzeshash raa daarad.
price this coat more than that one it is, but its worth D.O. it has.

(730) This dark chocolate contains only a little sugar.

این شکلات تلخ، فقط کمی شکر دارد.

in shokolaat_e talkh, faqat kami shekar daarad.
this chocolate bitter, only little sugar it has.

(731) This drawer contains paper, pens, pencils, and other things like that.

در این کشو کاغذ، خودکار، مداد و سایر چیزهای مشابه گذاشته شده است.

dar in kesho kaaqaz, khodkaar, medaad va saayer_e chizhaa_ye moshaabeh gozaashte shode ast.
in this drawer paper, pen, pencil and other things similar it has been put.

(732) This entrance is for staff only.

این ورودی فقط برای کارکنان است.

in vorudi faqat baraaye kaarkonaan ast.
this entrance only for staff it is.

(733) This hotel is particularly suitable for families with children.

این هتل مخصوصاً برای خانواده‌هایی که بچه دارند مناسب است.

in hotel makhsusan baraaye khaanevaadehaaiy ke bachche daarand monaaseb ast.
this hotel especially for families that child they have suitable it is.

(734)	یک معمار مشهور، این خانه را طراحی کرده است.	This house was designed by a famous architect.
	yek me'maar_e mashhur in khaane raa tarraahi karde ast	
	a famous architect this house D.O. s/he has designed	
(735)	این جواهرات مال مادربزرگم بوده است.	This jewelry was my grandmother's.
	in javaaherat maal_e maadarbozorgam bude ast	
	this jewelry property of my grandmother it has been	
(736)	این شغل به قدرت بدنی زیادی احتیاج دارد.	This job requires a lot of physical strength.
	in shoql be qodrat_e badani_ye ziyaadi ehtiyaaj daarad	
	this job to strength physical much need it has	
(737)	این فیلم در بین مردان بیشتر محبوب است تا در بین زنان.	This movie is more popular among men than women.
	in film dar beyn_e mardaan bishtar mahbub ast taa dar beyn_e zanaan	
	this movie between men more popular it is than at among women	
(738)	این فیلم فقط مخصوص بزرگسالان است. برای کودکان خیلی خشن است.	This movie is only for adults. It's too violent for children.
	in film faqat makhsus_e bozorgsaalaan ast baraaye kudakaan kheyli khashen ast	
	this movie only specific adults it is for children very violent it is	
(739)	این موسیقی در بین نوجوانان محبوب است.	This music is popular with teenagers.
	in musiqi dar beyn_e nojavaanaan mahbub ast	
	this music at among teenagers popular it is	
(740)	این اطلاعات جدید، ایده‌ای به من می‌دهد.	This new information gives me an idea.
	in ettelaa'aat_e jadid ideiy be man midahad	
	this information new an idea to I it gives	
(741)	این پماد باید سه بار در روز استفاده شود.	This ointment must be applied three times a day.
	in pomaad baayad se baar dar ruz estefaade shavad	
	this ointment must three time in day it should be used	
(742)	این بسته به آدرس اشتباه تحویل داده شده بود.	This package was delivered to the wrong address.
	in baste be aadres_e eshtebaah tahvil daade shode bud	
	this package to address wrong it had been delivered	

1000 Sentences

(743) This price is only available if you buy large quantities.

تنها در صورتی که به تعداد زیاد خرید کنید، می‌توانید
tanhaa — dar surati ke — be — te'daad_e ziyaad — kharid konid — mitavaanid
only — if — to — big number — you would buy — you can

از این قیمت ویژه استفاده کنید.
az — in — qeymat_e — vizhe — estefaade konid
from — this — price — special — you can use

(744) This report required a lot of research.

این گزارش به تحقیقات زیادی نیاز داشت.
in — gozaaresh — be — tahqiqaat_e — ziyaadi — niyaaz — daasht
this — report — to — research — much — need — it had

(745) This river flows into the Mediterranean Sea.

این رودخانه به دریای مدیترانه سرازیر می‌شود.
in — rudkhaane — be — daryaa_ye — meditaraane — saraazir mishavad
this — river — to — sea — Mediterranean — it flows

(746) This ship crosses the Atlantic Ocean twice per month.

این کشتی دو بار در ماه از اقیانوس اطلس
in — keshti — do baar — dar — maah — az — oqyanus_e — atlas
this — ship — twice — per — month — from — ocean — Atlantic

عبور می‌کند.
'obur mikonad
it crosses

(747) This shirt is not the right size for me. It's way too big.

اندازه‌ی این پیراهن به من نمی‌خورد. بیش از حد بزرگ
andaaze_ye — in — piraahan — be — man — nemikhorad — bish az hadd — bozorg
size — this — shirt — on — me — it doesn't fit — too — big

است.
ast
it is

(748) This song is very well known.

این آهنگ به خوبی شناخته شده است.
in — aahang — be khubi shenaakhte shode — ast
this — song — well known — it is

(749) This story is very famous. You have to read it.

این داستان خیلی معروف است. باید آن را بخوانی.
in — daastaan — kheyli — ma'ruf — ast — baayad — aan — raa — bekhaani
this — story — very — famous — it is — must — it — D.O. — you should read

(750) This sunscreen has a high sun protection factor (SPF).

ضریب محافظت (SPF) این کرم ضد آفتاب، مقابل
zarib_e — mohaafezat_e — (SPF) — in — kerem_e — zedd_e — aaftaab — moqaabel_e
factor — protection — (SPF) — this — cream — anti — sun — against

نور خورشید زیاد است.
nur_e — khorshid — ziyaad — ast
light — sun — high — it is

(751) This sweater is made of pure wool.

این پولوور از پشم خالص ساخته شده است.
in pulover az pashm_e khaales saakhte shode ast
this sweater from wool pure it has been made

(752) This tea should be steeped for 5 minutes in boiling water.

این چای باید به مدت پنج دقیقه در آب جوش دم بکشد.
in chaay baayad be moddat_e panj daqiqe dar aab_e jush dam bekeshad
this tea must for duration five minute at water boiling it should be steeped

(753) This time I would like to go to an island for vacation.

این بار دوست دارم برای تعطیلات به یک جزیره بروم.
in baar dust daaram baraaye ta'tilaat be yek jazire beravam
this time I like for vacation to a island I would go

(754) This train reaches a speed of 200 km/h.

سرعت این قطار به دویست کیلومتر در ساعت می‌رسد.
sor'at_e in qataar be devist kilumetr dar saa'at miresad
speed this train to two hundred kilometer per hour it reaches

(755) This vaccine protects you against flu.

این واکسن شما را در برابر آنفولانزا محافظت می‌کند.
in vaaksan shomaa raa dar baraabar_e aanfolaanzaa mohaafezat mikonad
this vaccine you against influenza it protects

(756) Thousands of people gathered to hear the president's speech.

هزاران نفر برای شنیدن سخنرانی رئیس‌جمهور جمع شدند.
hezaaraan nafar baraaye shenidan_e sokhanraani_ye raiysjomhur jam' shodand
thousands person for hearing speech president they gathered

(757) To highlight the word, simply double-click with the left mouse button.

برای هایلایت کردن کلمه، فقط کافیست با دکمه‌ی چپ ماوس، دو بار کلیک کنید.
baraaye haaylaayt kardan_e kaleme faqat kaafist baa dokme_ye chap_e maaws do baar kelik konid
for highlighting word only it's enough with button left mouse twice click

(758) Today is Monday, yesterday was Sunday, and tomorrow is Tuesday.

امروز دوشنبه است، دیروز یکشنبه بود و فردا
emruz doshanbe ast, diruz yekshanbe bud va fardaa
today Monday it is yesterday Sunday it was and tomorrow

سه‌شنبه است.
seshanbe ast
Tuesday it is

(759) Today's computers can do much more than a decade ago.

کامپیوترهای امروزی نسبت به یک دهه‌ی قبل،
kaampiyuterhaa_ye emruzi nesbat be yek dahe_ye qabl
computers today relative to a decade ago

می‌توانند کارهای بسیار بیشتری انجام دهند.
mitavaanand karhaa_ye besyaar bishtari anjaam dahand
they can activities much more they can do

(760) Tomorrow is my birthday. - How old will you be?

فردا تولدم است. - چند سالت می‌شود؟
fardaa tavallodam ast chand saalat mishavad
tomorrow my birthday it is how many your year it becomes

(761) Try to save at least twenty percent of your salary.

سعی کنید حداقل بیست درصد از حقوق خود را
sa'y konid haddeaqal bist darsad az hoquq_e khod raa
try at least twenty percent of salary self D.O.

پس‌انداز کنید.
pasandaaz konid
you would save

(762) Turn left at the next intersection.

در تقاطع بعدی به سمت چپ بپیچید.
dar taqato'_e ba'di be samt_e chap bepichid
at intersection next to direction left turn

(763) Turn off your cell phone before the movie starts.

قبل از شروع فیلم تلفن همراه خود را خاموش کنید.
qabl az shoru'_e film telefon_e hamraah_e khod raa khaamush konid
before start movie cell phone self D.O. turn off

(764) Unfortunately he can't enjoy the food because it is too spicy.

متأسفانه او نمی‌تواند از غذا لذت ببرد، چون
moteassefaane u nemitavaanad az qazaa lezzat bebarad, chon
unfortunately he he can't from food he could enjoy because

بیش از حد تند است.
bish az hadd tond ast
too spicy it is

(765) Unfortunately my bicycle broke down. I had to push it home.

متأسفانه دوچرخه‌ی من خراب شد. مجبور شدم تا
moteassefaane — unfortunately
docharkhe_ye man — my bicycle
kharaab shod — it broke
majbur shodam — I was forced
taa — until

خانه آن را هل بدهم.
khaane — home
aan — it
raa — D.O.
hol bedaham — I would push

(766) Unfortunately, you need to wait longer. - No problem. I don't mind.

متأسفانه باید بیشتر منتظر بمانید. – عیبی
moteassefaane — unfortunately
baayad — must
bishtar — more
montazer — waiting
bemaanid — you should remain
eybi — a problem

ندارد. مهم نیست.
nadaarad — it doesn't have
mohemm — important
nist — it is not

(767) Vacations during school holidays are always more expensive. This is peak season.

مسافرت در طول تعطیلات مدرسه همیشه گران است.
mosaaferat — travel
dar tul_e — during
ta'tilaat_e — holidays
madrese — school
hamishe — always
geraan — expensive
ast — it is

این فصل، فصل اوج گرفتن قیمت‌هاست.
in — this
fasl — season
fasl_e — season
owj gereftan_e — soaring
qeymathaast — (it is) prices

(768) Vegetables grow especially well in this soil.

به خصوص سبزیجات، در این خاک به خوبی
be khosus — especially
sabzijaat — vegetables
dar — in
in — this
khaak — soil
be khubi — well

رشد می‌کند.
roshd mikonad — it grows

(769) Vehicle emissions pollute the air.

گازهای خروجی وسایل نقلیه، هوا را آلوده می‌کند.
gaazhaa_ye — gases
khoruji_ye — output
vasaayel_e naqliyye — vehicles
havaa — air
raa — D.O.
aalude mikonad — it pollutes

(770) Vehicles are not allowed on this street. Pedestrians only.

ورود وسایل نقلیه به این خیابان مجاز نیست. فقط
vorud_e — entry
vasaayel_e naqliyye — vehicles
be — to
in — this
khiyaabaan — street
mojaaz — allowed
nist — it is not
faqat — only

عابران پیاده.
aaberaan_e piyaade — pedestrians

(771) War is still prevalent in this country.

جنگ همچنان در این کشور در جریان است.
jang — war
hamchenaan — still
dar — in
in — this
keshvar — country
dar jaryaan — ongoing
ast — it is

(772) Washing hands is good protection against getting sick.

شستن دست‌ها، محافظ خوبی در برابر بیمار شدن است.
shostan_e (washing) *dasthaa* (hands) *mohaafez_e* (protection) *khubi* (good) *dar baraabar_e* (against) *bimar* (sick) *shodan* (becoming) *ast* (it is)

(773) We absolutely must refuel. We have almost no gas left.

باید حتماً سوخت‌گیری کنیم. تقریباً هیچی بنزین نداریم.
baayad (must) *hatman* (absolutely) *sukhtgiri* (refueling) *konim* (we must do) *taqriban* (almost) *hichi* (none) *benzin* (gasoline) *nadaarim* (we don't have)

(774) We all hugged as we said goodbye.

همگی یکدیگر را بغل کرده و خداحافظی کردیم.
hamegi (all) *yekdigar* (each other) *raa* (D.O.) *baqal karde* (we hugged) *va* (and) *khodaahaafezi* (goodbye) *kardim* (we did)

(775) We always go for a walk after dinner.

همیشه پس از شام، برای قدم زدن می‌رویم.
hamishe (always) *pas az* (after) *shaam* (dinner) *baraaye* (for) *qadam zadan* (walking) *miravim* (we go)

(776) We are about the same age.

تقریباً همسن هستیم.
taqriban (almost) *hamsenn* (same age) *hastim* (we are)

(777) We are leaving at 8 o'clock sharp. Please be here on time.

دقیقاً ساعت هشت راه می‌افتیم. لطفاً به موقع اینجا باشید.
daqiqan (exactly) *saa'at_e* (hour) *hasht* (eight) *raah mioftim* (we leave) *lotfan* (please) *be* (on) *moqe'* (time) *injaa* (here) *baashid* (be)

(778) We are open every day except Saturday.

همه روزه به غیر از یکشنبه‌ها، باز هستیم.
hame (every) *ruze* (day) *be qeyr az* (besides) *yekshanbehaa* (Sundays) *baaz* (open) *hastim* (we are)

(779) We are sitting in the living room and watching TV.

در اتاق نشیمن نشسته‌ایم و تلویزیون تماشا می‌کنیم.
dar (at) *otaaq_e* (room) *neshiman* (sitting) *neshasteiym* (we have sit) *va* (and) *televizyun* (television) *tamaashaa mikonim* (we watch)

(780) We are staying at a hotel by the sea.

در هتلی در کنار دریا اقامت داریم.

dar	hoteli	dar kenaar_e	daryaa	eqaamat	daarim
at	a hotel	by	sea	accommodation	we have

(781) We bought a piece of land and want to build a house there.

تکه‌ای زمین خریده‌ایم و می‌خواهیم خانه‌ای در آنجا بسازیم.

tekkeiy	zamin	kharideiym	va	mikhaahim	khaaneiy	dar	aanjaa
a piece	land	we have bought	and	we want	a house	at	there

besaazim — we would build

(782) We bought ourselves a new couch and armchair.

یک کاناپه و صندلی راحتی جدیدی برای خودمان خریدیم.

yek	kaanaape	va	sandali_ye	raahati_ye	jadidi	baraaye	khodemaan
a	couch	and	chair	comfortable	new	for	ourselves

kharidim — we bought

(783) We came as quickly as we could.

تا آنجا که می‌توانستیم، سریع آمدیم.

taa	aanjaa	ke	mitavaanestim	sari'	aamadim
to	there	that	we were able	quick	we came

(784) We can meet tomorrow, however I am not free until after noon.

می‌توانیم فردا همدیگر را ببینیم، اما من تا

mitavaanim	fardaa	hamdigar	raa	bebinim	ammaa	man	taa
we can	tomorrow	each other	D.O.	we can see	but	I	until

بعد از ظهر وقت آزاد ندارم.

ba'd az	zohr	vaqt_e	aazaad	nadaaram
after	noon	time	free	I don't have

(785) We chatted about the political debate.

دربارهٔ مناظرهٔ سیاسی گپ زدیم.

darbaare_ye	monaazere_ye	siyaasi	gap zadim
about	debate	political	we chatted

(786) We congratulate you on the birth of your child!

تولد فرزندتان را به شما تبریک می‌گوییم!

tavallod_e	farzandetaan	raa	be	shomaa	tabrik	miguiym
birth	your child	D.O.	to	you	congratulations	we say

(787) **We decided to buy a smaller, more fuel-efficient car.**

تصمیم گرفتیم که یک ماشین کوچک‌تر، با مصرف بنزین بهینه‌تر بخریم.

tasmim gereftim ke yek maashin kuchektar, baa masraf_e benzin_e behinetar bekharim.
we decided that a car smaller with consumption gas more efficient we should buy

(788) **We don't eat meat. We are vegetarian.**

ما گوشت نمی‌خوریم. گیاهخواریم.

maa gusht nemikhorim. giyaahkhaarim.
we meat we don't eat. we're vegetarian.

(789) **We don't have enough space in our small apartment.**

در آپارتمان کوچک خود، فضای کافی نداریم.

dar aapaartemaan_e kuchak_e khod, fazaa_ye kaafi nadaarim.
at apartment small self, space enough we don't have.

(790) **We got married in 1990.**

ما در سال هزار و نهصد و نود ازدواج کردیم.

maa dar saal_e hezaar o nohsad o navad ezdevaaj kardim.
we at year thousand and nine hundred and ninety we got married.

(791) **We have a nice, big vegetable garden.**

ما یک باغ سبزیجات زیبا و بزرگ داریم.

maa yek baaq_e sabzijaat_e zibaa va bozorg daarim.
we a garden vegetable beautiful and big we have.

(792) **We have a TV with a very large screen.**

ما یک تلویزیون با صفحه نمایش بسیار بزرگ داریم.

maa yek televizyun baa safhe_ye namaayesh_e besyaar bozorg daarim.
we a television with screen display very big we have.

(793) **We have been living in this apartment since 2016.**

ما از سال دو هزار و شانزده، در این آپارتمان زندگی می‌کنیم.

maa az saal_e do hezaar o shaanzdah, dar in aapaartemaan zendegi mikonim.
we since year two thousand and sixteen, in this apartment we live.

(794) **We have gotten used to life in this country.**

ما به زندگی در این کشور عادت کرده‌ایم.

maa be zendegi dar in keshvar 'aadat kardeiym.
we to life at this country we have got used to.

(795) صندلی‌های خیلی خوبی داریم - وسط ردیف چهارم.

We have great seats - middle of the fourth row.

chahaarom radif_e vasat_e daarim khubi kheyli sandalihaa_ye
fourth row middle we have good very seats

(796) نه وقت تعطیلات را داریم و نه پولش را.

We have neither time nor money for vacation.

raa pulash na va daarim raa ta'tilaat vaqt_e na
D.O. its money no and we have D.O. vacation time no

(797) دیگر چوبی برای آتش نداریم.

We have no more wood for the fire.

nadaarim aatash baraaye chubi digar
we don't have fire for wood no longer

(798) نقاش گرفته‌ایم تا دیوارها را دوباره نقاشی کنیم.

We have the painters in the house because we are having the walls repainted.

naqqaashi konim dobaare raa divaarhaa taa gerefteiym naqqaash
we would paint again D.O. walls so we have got painter

(799) این لباس را در چندین رنگ مختلف داریم.

We have this dress in several different colors.

daarim mokhtalef rang_e chandin dar raa lebaas in
we have different color several in D.O. cloth this

(800) باید شما را معاینه کنیم. ممکن است که صدمات داخلی داشته باشید.

We have to examine you. It might be that you have internal injuries.

sadamaat_e ke ast momken mo'aayene konim shomaa raa baayad
injuries that it is possible we should examine you must

daashte baashid daakheli
you may have internal

(801) باید الان برویم، وگرنه خیلی دیر خواهد شد.

We have to go now, otherwise it will be too late.

khaahad shod dir kheyli vagarna beravim alaan baayad
it will become late very otherwise we should go now must

(802) باید سقف را تعمیر کنیم.

We have to have the roof repaired.

ta'miyr konim raa saqf baayad
we should repair D.O. roof must

(803) ما باید عجله کنیم. در غیر این صورت قطار را از دست خواهیم داد.

We have to hurry. Otherwise we'll miss the train.

raa qataar dar qeyr_e in surat 'ajale konim baayad maa
D.O. train otherwise we should hurry must we

az dast khaahim daad
we will miss

(804) We have to operate on your foot immediately.

ما باید فوراً پای شما را عمل کنیم.

maa baayad foran paa_ye shomaa raa 'amal konim
we must immediately your foot D.O. we should operate

(805) We have to separate the garbage from the recycling.

ما باید زباله‌ها را از بازیافتی‌ها جدا کنیم.

maa baayad zobaalehaa raa az baazyaaftihaa jodaa konim
we must trashes D.O. from recyclables we should separate

(806) We have too few players. We need one more.

خیلی کم بازیکن داریم. یک نفر دیگر لازم داریم.

kheyli kam baazikon daarim yek nafar_e digar laazem daarim
very few player we have a person another need we have

(807) We have two adult daughters.

ما دو دختر بالغ داریم.

maa do dokhtar_e baaleq daarim
we two daughter adult we have

(808) We have two trees in front of our house.

دو درخت در جلوی خانه‌مان داریم.

do derakht dar jelo_ye khaanemaan daarim
two tree in front our house we have

(809) We have very good working conditions in our company.

ما شرایط کاری بسیار خوبی در شرکت‌مان داریم.

maa sharaayet_e kaari_ye besyaar khubi dar sherkatemaan daarim
we condition working very good in our company we have

(810) We haven't seen each other for a long time. - Yes, that was really long ago.

مدتهاست که یکدیگر را ندیده‌ایم. - بله، واقعاً

moddathaast ke yekdigar raa nadideiym bale vaaqe'an
(it is) a long time that each other D.O. we have not seen yes really

خیلی وقت پیش بود.

kheyli vaqt pish bud
very time ago it was

(811) We just sat down to eat breakfast.

ما فقط نشستیم تا صبحانه بخوریم.

maa faqat neshastim taa sobhaane bokhorim
we just we sat so breakfast we would eat

(812) We landed two hours late.

دو ساعت دیر فرود آمدیم.

do saa'at dir forud aamadim
two hour late we landed

(813) We left the light on all night.

تمام طول شب چراغ را روشن گذاشتیم.

tamaam_e tul_e shab cheraaq raa roshan gozaashtim
all duration night light D.O. on we put

(814) We like them because they are so funny.

ما آنها را دوست داریم، چون خیلی بامزه هستند.
maa aanhaa raa dust daarim chon kheyli baamazze hastand
we them we like because very funny they are

(815) We live in a nice neighborhood.

ما در یک محله‌ی خوب زندگی می‌کنیم.
maa dar yek mahalle_ye khub zendegi mikonim
we in a neighborhood good we live

(816) We live on the second floor, and my parents live on the floor above us.

ما در طبقه‌ی دوم زندگی می‌کنیم و والدینم در طبقه‌ی بالای ما زندگی می‌کنند.
maa dar tabaqe_ye dovvom zendegi mikonim va vaaledeynam dar tabaqe_ye baalaa_ye maa zendegi mikonand
we at floor second we live and my parents at floor above we they live

(817) We live outside of the city.

ما در خارج از شهر زندگی می‌کنیم.
maa dar khaarej az shahr zendegi mikonim
we at out of city we live

(818) We live upstairs on the 4th floor.

ما در طبقه چهارم زندگی می‌کنیم.
maa dar tabaqe_ye chahaarom zendegi mikonim
we at floor fourth we live

(819) We lived abroad for a long time, but now we are back.

مدت زیادی خارج از کشور زندگی کردیم، اما حالا برگشته‌ایم.
moddat_e ziyaadi khaarej az keshvar zendegi kardim ammaa haalaa bargashteiym
time long out of country we lived but now we have returned

(820) We lost the last few games. Thankfully we won this time.

چند بازی آخر را باختیم. خوشبختانه این بار بردیم.
chand baazi_ye aakhar raa baakhtim khoshbakhtaane in baar bordim
few game last D.O. we lost fortunately this time we won

(821) We need a creative solution to this problem because the standard solutions aren't working.	ما برای حل این مشکل، به یک راه حل خلاقانه نیاز داریم، چون راه‌حل‌های استاندارد جواب نمی‌دهند.	maa baraaye hall_e in moshkel, be yek raah_e hall_e khallaaqaane niyaaz daarim, chon raah_e halhaa_ye estaandaard javaab nemidahand.
(822) We need another fork, please.	ما یک چنگال دیگر لازم داریم، لطفاً.	maa yek changaal_e digar laazem daarim, lotfan.
(823) We need lots of candles for your birthday cake. You are old.	برای کیک تولد شما به شمع‌های زیادی احتیاج داریم. شما پیر هستید.	baraaye keyk_e tavallod_e shomaa be sham'haa_ye ziyaadi ehtiyaaj daarim. shomaa pir hastid.
(824) We need the following details from you: name, address, date of birth.	ما به این اطلاعات از شما نیاز داریم: نام، آدرس، تاریخ تولد.	maa be in ettelaa'aat az shomaa niyaaz daarim: naam, aadres, taarikh_e tavallod.
(825) We need three to four weeks for the renovation.	برای نوسازی به سه تا چهار هفته زمان نیاز داریم.	baraaye nosaazi be se taa chahaar hafte zamaan niyaaz daarim.
(826) We only have a small apartment, but we are happy with it.	ما فقط یک آپارتمان کوچک داریم، اما از آن راضی هستیم.	maa faqat yek aapaartemaan_e kuchak daarim, ammaa az aan raazi hastim.
(827) We own the business together. We are partners.	ما با یکدیگر کسب و کار داریم. ما شریک هم هستیم.	maa baa yekdigar kasb o kaar daarim. maa sharik_e ham hastim.

1000 Sentences

(828) We plan to go to Portugal for our upcoming vacation.

ما قصد داریم برای تعطیلات پیش روی خود، به پرتغال برویم.
maa qasd daarim baraaye ta'tilaat_e pish_e ru_ye khod be porteqaal beravim.
we intention we have for vacation upcoming self to Portugal we would go

(829) We really wanted to visit friends, but then we just stayed home.

واقعاً می‌خواستیم دوستان را ببینیم، اما فقط خانه ماندیم.
vaaqe'an mikhaastim dustaan raa bebinim, ammaa faqat khaane maandim.
really we were wanting friends D.O. we would see but only home we stayed

(830) We received your letter dated January 3rd.

نامه‌ی شما به تاریخ سوم ژانویه را دریافت کردیم.
naame_ye shomaa be taarikh_e sevvom_e zhaanviye raa daryaaft kardim.
your letter to date third January D.O. we received

(831) We spent our vacation in the mountains.

تعطیلات خود را در کوهستان گذراندیم.
ta'tilaat_e khod raa dar kuhestaan gozaraandim.
vacation self D.O. at mountain we spent (time)

(832) We still have to discuss exactly when we're leaving and what we're taking with us.

ما باید دقیقاً در مورد اینکه کی می‌رویم و چه چیزی باید با خود برداریم، صحبت کنیم.
maa baayad daqiqan dar mored_e inke key miravim va che chizi baayad baa khod bardaarim, sohbat konim.
we must exactly about that when we go and what thing must with self we should pick up we would speak

(833) We still have twenty minutes until departure.

هنوز بیست دقیقه تا زمان رفتن وقت داریم.
hanuz bist daqiqe taa zamaan_e raftan vaqt daarim.
still twenty minute until time going time we have

(834) We took the long way home.

ما راهی طولانی تا خانه داشتیم.
maa raahi tulaani taa khaane daashtim.
we way long to home we had

(835) We unfortunately can't come to an agreement.

متأسفانه ما نمی‌توانیم به توافق برسیم.
moteassefaane maa nemitavaanim be tavaafoq beresim.
unfortunately we we can't to agreement we would reach

(836) We usually go abroad on vacation.

ما معمولاً برای تعطیلات به خارج از کشور می‌رویم.

maa ma'mulan baraaye ta'tilaat be khaarej az keshvar miravim
we / usually / for / vacation / to / outside / of / country / we go

(837) We want the freedom to speak our minds.

ما می‌خواهیم آزادانه در مورد افکارمان صحبت کنیم.

maa mikhaahim aazaadaane dar mored_e afkaaremaan sohbat konim
we / we want / freely / about / our thoughts / we would speak

(838) We want to build a house and are looking for a cheap plot of land.

ما می‌خواهیم خانه‌ای بسازیم و به دنبال یک

maa mikhaahim khaaneiy besaazim va be donbaal_e yek
we / we want / a house / we would build / and / ←looking for / a

زمین ارزان‌قیمت هستیم.

zamin_e arzaanqeymat hastim
land / cheap / we are→

(839) We want to buy our teacher a gift. Who would like to join in?

ما می‌خواهیم برای معلممان هدیه بخریم. کی

maa mikhaahim baraaye mo'allememaan hadiye bekharim ki
we / we want / for / our teacher / gift / we would buy / who

دوست دارد در این کار شریک باشد؟

dust daarad dar in kaar sharik baashad
s/he likes / at / this / activity / partner / s/he would be

(840) We want to give you something for your birthday.

ما می‌خواهیم برای تولدتان چیزی به شما

maa mikhaahim baraaye tavallodetaan chizi be shomaa
we / we want / for / your birthday / something / to / you

بدهیم.

bedahim
we would give

(841) We want to spend the night outdoors under the moon and stars.

ما می‌خواهیم شب را بیرون از خانه و زیر ماه و

maa mikhaahim shab raa birun az khaane va zir_e maah va
we / we want / night / D.O. / outside / of / home / and / under / moon / and

ستاره‌ها بگذرانیم.

setaarehaa begozaraanim
stars / we would spend (time)

(842) We were friends as children, but we don't like each other as adults.

ما در کودکی با هم دوست بودیم، اما در بزرگ‌سالی

maa dar kudaki baa ham dust budim ammaa dar bozorgsaali
we / in / childhood / together / friend / we were / but / in / adulthood

از یکدیگر خوشمان نمی‌آید.

az yekdigar khoshemaan nemiaayad
from / each other / we don't like

(843) We will advise you in legal matters.
ما در امور حقوقی، به شما مشاوره خواهیم داد.
maa dar omur_e hoquqi, be shomaa moshaavere khaahim daad
we in affairs legal to you advice we will give

(844) We'll this apartment for a year and then move somewhere else.
ما یک سال دیگر در این آپارتمان می‌نشینیم و بعد به جای دیگری خواهیم رفت.
maa yek saal_e digar dar in aapaartemaan mineshinim va ba'd be jaa_ye digari khaahim raft
we a year another in this apartment we sit and then to place another we will go

(845) We're going camping, so we're taking a tent with us.
قرار است به اردو برویم، بنابراین با خودمان چادر می‌بریم.
qaraar ast be ordu beravim, banaabarin baa khodemaan chaador mibarim
it is arranged to camp we may go thus with ourselves tent we take

(846) We're going on vacation with some friends. It should be fun.
قرار است به همراه چند دوست به تعطیلات برویم. باید خوش بگذرد.
qaraar ast be hamraah_e chand dust be ta'tilaat beravim. baayad khosh begozarad
it is arranged along with several friend to vacation we may go. must good it should pass

(847) We're looking for an apartment in a central location.
ما به دنبال یک آپارتمان هستیم که موقعیت مرکزی داشته باشد.
maa be donbaal_e yek aapaartemaan hastim ke moqe'iyyat_e markazi daashte baashad
we looking for a apartment we are that situation central it would have

(848) We're now flying at an altitude of 10,000 m.
اکنون در ارتفاع ده هزار متری پرواز می‌کنیم.
aknun dar ertefaa'_e dah hezaar metri parvaaz mikonim
now at height ten thousand meter we fly

(849) We're putting the bookcase here in the corner.
ما قفسه‌ی کتاب‌ها را اینجا، در این گوشه، قرار می‌دهیم.
maa qafase_ye ketaabhaa raa injaa dar in gushe, qaraar midahim
we shelf books D.O. here at this corner we put

We're staying only until tomorrow.	ما فقط تا فردا می‌مانیم.	maa faqat taa fardaa mimaanim	we only until tomorrow we stay	(850)
We're taking a break once we reach the top of the hill.	وقتی به بالای تپه برسیم، استراحت می‌کنیم.	vaqti be baalaa_ye tappe beresim, esteraahat mikonim	when to top hill we would arrive, we rest	(851)
We're taking a ferry to the island.	ما با کشتی تفریحی به جزیره می‌رویم.	maa baa keshti_ye tafrihi be jazire miravim	we with ship recreational to island we go	(852)
We're visiting my in-laws tomorrow.	فردا خویشاوندان سببی خود را خواهیم دید.	fardaa khishaavandaan_e sababi_ye khod raa khaahim did	tomorrow in-laws self D.O. we will see	(853)
What a coincidence meeting you here.	چه تصادفی که شما را اینجا دیدم.	che tasaadofi ke shomaa raa injaa didam	what accident that you D.O. here I saw	(854)
What a cute baby!	چه بچه‌ی نازی!	che bachche_ye naazi	what baby cute	(855)
What a thunderstorm! Did you see the lightning and hear the thunder?	چه رعد و برقی! برق را دیدی و رعد را شنیدی؟	che ra'd o barqi! barq raa didi va ra'd raa shenidi	what thunder and lightning! the lightning D.O. you saw and thunder D.O. you heard	(856)
What are you laughing at?	به چه داری می‌خندی؟	be che daari mikhandi	to what you are laughing	(857)
What are your monthly expenses?	خرج شما ماهانه چقدر است؟	kharj_e shomaa maahaane cheqadr ast	your expense monthly how much it is	(858)
What color is currently fashionable?	الان چه رنگی مد روز است؟	alaan che rangi mod_e ruz ast	now what color fashionable it is	(859)
What day do I have to return the book to the library?	چه روزی باید این کتاب را به کتابخانه پس بدهم؟	che ruzi baayad in ketaab raa be ketaabkhaane pas bedaham	what day must this book D.O. to library I should return	(860)

(861) What day is today?

امروز چه روزی است؟
emruz che ruzi ast
today what day it is

(862) What did the man say? I only understood half.

آن مرد چه گفت؟ من فقط نیمی از حرف‌هایش را
aan mard che goft? man faqat nimi az harfhaayaash raa
that man what he said I only half of his talks D.O.

فهمیدم.
fahmidam
I understood

(863) What do we need for the party? - Make a shopping list.

برای مهمانی چه چیزهایی لازم داریم؟ - یک لیست
baraaye mehmaani che chizhaaiy laazem daarim yek list_e
for party what things need you have a list

خرید بنویس.
kharid benevis
shopping write

(864) What do you do for a living?

شغلت چیست؟
shoqlat chist
your job it is what

(865) What do you want for your birthday?

برای تولدت چه چیزی می‌خواهی؟
baraaye tavallodat che chizi mikhaahi
for your birthday what thing you want

(866) What does this word mean? - Look it up in a dictionary.

معنی این کلمه چیست؟ - در فرهنگ لغت، آن را
ma'ni_ye in kaleme chist? dar farhang_e loqat aan raa
meaning this word it is what in dictionary it D.O.

پیدا کن.
peydaa kon
find

(867) What is the name of this river?

نام این رودخانه چیست؟
naam_e in rudkhaane chist
name this river what is it

(868) What is wrong? Are you in pain?

چه مشکلی پیش آمده است؟ آیا درد داری؟
che moshkeli pish aamade ast aayaa dard daari
what problem it has occurred I.P. pain you have

(869) What is your native language?

زبان مادری تو چیست؟
zabaan_e maadari_ye to chist
language your mother what is it

What is your wife's first name?	اسم کوچک همسرت چیست؟ *esm_e kuchak_e hamsarat chist* name small your wife what is it	(870)
What is your wi-fi password?	رمز عبور وایفای شما چیست؟ *ramz_e 'obur_e waayfaay_e shomaa chist* password your wi-fi what is it	(871)
What kind of car do you have? - I don't have one.	چه نوع ماشینی دارید؟ - من ماشین ندارم. *che no' maashini daarid man maashin nadaaram* what type a car you have I car I don't have	(872)
What kind of music do you like to listen to?	چه نوع موسیقی دوست داری گوش بدهی؟ *che no' musiqi dust daari gush bedahi* what type music you like you would listen to	(873)
What would you do if you were me?	اگر جای من بودی، چکار می‌کردی؟ *agar jaa_ye man budi chekaar mikardi* if my place you were what would you do	(874)
When and where were you born?	کی و کجا متولد شده‌اید؟ *key va kojaa motevalled shodeiyd* when and where you have been born	(875)
When are we meeting? - Around 10 o'clock. Is that okay for you?	چه موقع همدیگر را ببینیم؟ - حدود ساعت ده. برای *che moqe' hamdigar raa bebinim hodud_e saa'at_e dah baraaye* what time each other D.O. we may see around hour ten for شما مناسب است؟ *shomaa monaaseb ast* you suitable it is	(876)
When do we find out the result of the (medical) test?	چه موقع نتیجه آزمایش (پزشکی) را می‌فهمیم؟ *che moqe' natije aazmaayesh_e pezeshki raa mifahmim* what time result test (medical) D.O. we find out	(877)
When Dr. Levi was on vacation, I went to the person who was covering for him.	وقتی دکتر لوی در تعطیلات بود، پیش شخصی رفتم *vaqti doktor levi dar ta'tilaat bud pish_e shakhsi raftam* when doctor Levi at vacation he was to a person I went که کارهای او را انجام می‌داد. *ke kaarhaa_ye u raa anjaam midaad* that his works D.O. he was doing	(878)

(879)	When I turn 18, I'll have a big party.	وقتی هجده ساله بشوم، مهمانی بزرگی vaqti hejdah saal_e beshavam, mehmaani_ye bozorgi when eighteen year I would become party big برگزار خواهم کرد. bargozaar khaaham kard I will hold
(880)	When I was 15 years old, I really wanted to learn to play piano. But I had no money for it back then.	وقتی پانزده سال داشتم، واقعاً دوست داشتم پیانو vaqti paanzdah saal daashtam, vaaqe'an dust daashtam piyaano when fifteen year I had really I liked piano بزنم، اما آن زمان پول برای آن نداشتم. bezanam, ammaa aan zamaan pul baraaye aan nadaashtam I would play but that time money for that I didn't have
(881)	When I'm finished at work, I'm going home.	هر وقت کارم تمام شود، به خانه می‌روم. har vaqt kaaram tamaam shavad, be khaane miravam when my work it may be finished to home I go
(882)	When should I come? Is tomorrow evening okay with you?	چه زمانی باید بیایم؟ آیا فردا عصر برای che zamaani baayad biyaayam? aayaa fardaa 'asr baraaye what time must I should come I.P. tomorrow evening for شما مناسب است؟ shomaa monaaseb ast you suitable it is
(883)	When the kids are grown, we will have more free time again.	وقتی بچه‌ها بزرگ شوند، دوباره وقت آزادتری vaqti bachchehaa bozorg shavand, dobaare vaqt_e aazaadtari when kids big they would become again time more free خواهیم داشت. khaahim daasht we will have
(884)	When was the last time you saw your family?	آخرین باری که خانواده خود را دیدید، کی بود؟ aakharin baari ke khaanevaade_ye khod raa didid, key bud last time that family self D.O. you saw when it was
(885)	When was the last time you went to the dentist?	آخرین باری که پیش دندانپزشک رفتید، کی بود؟ aakharin baari ke pish_e dandaanpezeshk raftid, key bud last time that to dentist you went when it was

(886)	When we got home, the kids were already fast asleep.	وقتی به خانه رسیدیم، بچه‌ها دیگر خوابشان برده بود. vaqti be khaane residim bachchehaa digar khaabeshaan borde bud when to home we arrived kids anymore they had fallen asleep
(887)	Where are you from? - From France.	شما اهل کجا هستید؟ - اهل فرانسه. shomaa ahl_e kojaa hastid ahl_e faraanse you from where you are from France
(888)	Where are you spending the night? - At a youth hostel.	شب را کجا می‌مانی؟ - در یک خوابگاه جوانان. shab raa kojaa mimaani dar yek khaabgaah_e javaanaan night D.O. where you stay at a youth hostel
(889)	Where are your so-called friends tonight?	آن به اصطلاح دوستانتان، امشب کجا هستند؟ aan be estelaah dustanetaan emshab kojaa hastand that so-called your friends tonight where they are
(890)	Where do you want to sit - outside or inside?	کجا می‌خواهید بنشینید - بیرون یا داخل؟ kojaa mikhaahid beneshinid birun yaa daakhel where you want you would sit outside or inside
(891)	Where is the toilet? - Go up the stairs and then left.	دستشویی کجاست؟ - از پله‌ها بالا رفته و سپس dastshuyi kojaast az pellehaa baalaa rafte va sepas restroom/W.C. where is it from stairs up go and then به سمت چپ بروید. be samt_e chap beravid towards left go
(892)	Where on your computer did you save the file?	این فایل را در کجای کامپیوترتان ذخیره می‌کنید؟ in faayl raa dar kojaa_ye kaampiyuteretaan zakhire mikonid this file D.O. at where your computer you save
(893)	Where should I send my application?	درخواست خود را به کجا باید ارسال کنم؟ darkhaast_e khod raa be kojaa baayad ersaal konam application self D.O. to where must I should send
(894)	Where would you like to sit? In the back or in front?	کجا دوست دارید بنشینید؟ عقب یا جلو؟ kojaa dust daarid beneshinid 'aqab yaa jelo where you like you would sit back or front
(895)	Which diseases should I get vaccinated against?	برای کدام بیماری‌ها باید واکسن بزنم؟ baraaye kodaam bimaarihaa baayad vaaksan bezanam for which diseases must vaccination I should hit
(896)	Which pants are you wearing tonight? - These here.	امشب کدام شلوار را می‌پوشی؟ - این که اینجاست. emshab kodaam shalvaar raa mipushi in ke injaast tonight which pants D.O. you wear this that it's here

(897) **Which shirt looks better on me?**

کدام پیراهن بیشتر به من می‌آید؟
kodaam piraahan bishtar be man miaayad
which shirt more to I it comes

(898) **Who fills in for you when you are on vacation?**

وقتی به تعطیلات می‌روی، چه کسی کار تو را انجام می‌دهد؟
vaqti be ta'tilaat miravi, che kasi kaar_e to raa anjaam midahad
when to holidays you go what person your work D.O. s/he does

(899) **Who ripped the page out of the book?**

چه کسی صفحه‌ی کتاب را پاره کرد؟
che kasi safhe_ye ketaab raa paare kard
what person page book D.O. s/he tore off

(900) **Who told you the secret?**

چه کسی آن راز را به تو گفت؟
che kasi aan raaz raa be to goft
what person that secret D.O. to you s/he said

(901) **Who will take care of the children while we're on vacation?**

وقتی به تعطیلات برویم، کی از بچه‌ها مراقبت می‌کند؟
vaqti be ta'tilaat beravim, ki az bachchehaa moraaqebat mikonad
when to vacation we would go who of children s/he takes care

(902) **Who's next in line?**

نفر بعدی در صف کیست؟
nafar_e ba'di dar saf kist
person next in line who is it

(903) **Who's there? - It's me.**

چه کسی آنجاست؟ - منم.
che kasi aanjaast manam
what individual it's there it's me

(904) **Why are you never happy?**

چرا هیچ‌وقت خوشحال نیستی؟
cheraa hichvaqt khoshhaal nisti
why never happy you are not

(905) **Why are you only wearing such a light coat? It is cold outside.**

چرا فقط کتی به این نازکی پوشیده‌ای؟ بیرون سرد است.
cheraa faqat koti be in naazoki pushide'i birun sard ast
why only a coat such thin you have worn outside cold it is

(906) Why didn't you come? I waited specially for you.
چرا نیامدی؟ من مخصوصاً منتظر تو بودم.
cheraa nayaamadi? man makhsusan montazer_e to budam.
why you didn't come I specially waiting you I was

(907) Why didn't you go to the doctor right away?
چرا فوری دکتر نرفتی؟
cheraa fori doktor narafti?
why immediately doctor you didn't go

(908) Why have not you been in touch for so long? Have you been ill?
چرا این مدت طولانی در تماس نبودید؟ مریض شده‌اید؟
cheraa in moddat_e tulaani dar tamaas nabudid? mariz shodeiyd?
why this time long in contact you were not sick you have become

(909) Why isn't the elevator coming? - You have to press the button.
چرا آسانسور نمی‌آید؟ - شما باید این دکمه را فشار دهید.
cheraa aasaansor nemiaayad? shomaa baayad in dokme raa feshaar dahid.
why elevator it doesn't come you must this button D.O. you should press

(910) Will it take long? - It may take an hour or so.
خیلی طول می‌کشد؟ - ممکن است یک ساعت یا بیشتر طول بکشد.
kheyli tul mikeshad? momken ast yek saa'at yaa bishtar tul bekeshad.
very it takes a long time possible it is an hour or more it may take a long time

(911) Will you come for a walk? - I would like to, but I have to work.
برای پیاده‌روی می‌آیید؟ - خیلی دوست دارم، اما باید کار کنم.
baraaye piyaaderavi miyaaiyd? kheyli dust daaram, ammaa baayad kaar konam.
for walking you come very I like but must I should work

(912) Will you give me a bowl for the salad, please?
لطفاً یک کاسه برای سالاد، به من می‌دهی؟
lotfan yek kaase baraaye saalaad, be man midahiy?
please a bowl for salad to I you give

(913) Will you help me to decorate the table for the party?
به من برای تزیین میز مهمانی کمک می‌کنی؟
be man baraaye taziyn_e miz_e mehmaani komak mikoni?
to I for decoration table party you help

(914)	Will you help me with my application?	به من برای فرم درخواستم کمک می‌کنی؟ *be man baraaye form_e darkhaastam komak mikoni* to I for form my application you help
(915)	Will you please bring extra batteries for the camera?	می‌توانی لطفاً باتری اضافه برای دوربین بیاوری؟ *mitavaani lotfan baatri_ye ezaafe baraaye durbin biyaavari* you can please battery additional for camera you can bring
(916)	Will you send me a postcard while you're on vacation?	میشه وقتی در تعطیلات هستی، برای من کارت پستال بفرستی؟ *mishe vaqti dar ta'tilaat hasti, baraaye man kaart postaal befresti* it is possible when at vacation you are for I card postal you can send
(917)	Winter was colder than normal.	زمستان سردتر از حد معمول بود. *zemestaan sardtar az hadd_e ma'mul bud* winter colder than normal it was
(918)	Wish me luck!	برای من آرزوی موفقیت کنید. *baraaye man aarezu_ye movafaqiyyat konid* for I wish success do
(919)	With a good education you will surely find a job.	با تحصیلات خوب، مطمئناً شغلی پیدا خواهید کرد. *baa tahsilaat_e khub, motma'ennan shoqli peydaa khaahid kard* with education good surely a job you will find
(920)	With a higher income you must pay more taxes.	با داشتن درآمد بالاتر، باید مالیات بیشتری پرداخت کنی. *baa daashtan_e daraamad_e baalaatar, baayad maaliyaat_e bishtari pardaakht koni* with having income higher must taxes more you must pay
(921)	With cars you have to check the oil regularly.	باید به طور منظم، روغن ماشین‌ها را بررسی کنید. *baayad be tor_e monazzam, roqan_e maashinhaa raa barresi konid* must in way regular oil cars D.O. you should check
(922)	Without my family I feel a little bit lonely.	بدون خانواده‌ام کمی احساس تنهایی می‌کنم. *bedun_e khaanevaadeam kami ehsaas_e tanhaayi mikonam* without my family a little feeling alone I do
(923)	Women are in the minority in our company.	در شرکت ما، زنان در اقلیت هستند. *dar sherkat_e maa, zanaan dar aqalliyyat hastand* at our company in women in minority they are

Would you like an egg for breakfast?	برای صبحانه، تخم مرغ می‌خواهید؟ mikhaahid morq tokhm_e sobhaane baraaye you want chicken egg breakfast for	(924)
Would you like anything else to eat? - No thanks, I'm full.	دوست دارید چیز دیگری بخورید؟ - نه ممنون، من man mamnun na bokhorid digari chiz_e dust daarid I thanks no you may eat else something you like سیر شدم. shodam sir I became full	(925)
Would you like some fruit? The pears are quite nice today.	میوه می‌خواهید؟ گلابی‌های امروز، خیلی خوب هستند. hastand khub kheyli emruz golaabihaa_ye mikhaahid mive they are good very today pears you want fruit	(926)
Would you prefer to live in the countryside or in the city?	ترجیح می‌دهید در شهر زندگی کنید یا در حومه‌ی آن؟ aan home_ye dar yaa zendegi konid shahr dar tarjih midahid that outskirt in or you would live city in you prefer	(927)
Would you spell your name please?	می‌شود لطفاً اسم خود را هجی کنید؟ hejji konid raa khod esm_e lotfan mishavad you would spell D.O. self name please it is possible	(928)
Yesterday I deposited money in my bank account.	دیروز پول را به حساب بانکی خود واریز کردم. vaariz kardam khod baanki_ye hesaab_e be raa pul diruz I deposited self bank account in D.O. money yesterday	(929)
Yesterday our new neighbor spoke to me in the stairwell.	دیروز همسایه جدیدمان، در راه پله، با من man baa raah pelle dar jadidemaan hamsaaye_ye diruz I with staircase at our new neighbor yesterday صحبت کرد. sohbat kard s/he spoke	(930)
Yesterday there was a discussion on television on the topic of immigration.	دیروز در تلویزیون بحثی با موضوع مهاجرت mohaajerat mozu_e baa bahsi televiziyun dar diruz immigration topic with a discussion television at yesterday ارائه شد. eraae shod it was presented	(931)

(932) **Yesterday we got lost in the woods. We didn't find the right way until an hour later.**
دیروز در جنگل گم شدیم. تا یک ساعت بعد، راه درست را پیدا نکردیم.
diruz dar jangal gom shodim. taa yek saa'at_e ba'd, raah_e dorost raa peydaa nakardim.
yesterday in woods we got lost until a hour later way right D.O. we didn't find

(933) **You absolutely must have the brakes checked.**
شما حتماً باید می‌دادید ترمزها را بررسی می‌کردند.
shomaa hatman baayad midaadiyd tormozhaa raa barresi mikardand.
you certainly must you were giving brakes D.O. they were checking

(934) **You absolutely must register in advance for this course.**
شما حتماً باید از قبل، برای این دوره ثبت‌نام کنید.
shomaa hatman baayad az qabl, baraaye in dowre sabtenaam konid.
you certainly must from before for this course you should register

(935) **You are allowed to take luggage weighing up to 20 kg.**
شما مجازید تا حداکثر بیست کیلوگرم بار مسافر داشته باشید.
shomaa mojaazid taa hadeaksar bist kilogeram baar_e mosaafer daashte baashid.
you you are allowed up to maximum twenty kilogram load passenger you may have

(936) **You are here too! What a coincidence!**
شما هم اینجا هستید! چه تصادفی!
shomaa ham injaa hastid che tasaadofi
you too here you are what coincidence

(937) **You are surely tired. - No, quite the contrary.**
حتماً خسته هستی. - نه، کاملاً برعکس.
hatman khaste hasti na kaamelan bar'aks
surely tired you are no completely contrary

(938) **You are wrong. Their daughter is 16, not 14.**
تو اشتباه می‌کنی. دخترشان شانزده سال دارد، نه چهارده سال.
to eshtebaah mikoni dokhtareshaan shaanzdah saal daarad, na chahaardah saal.
you you make mistake their daughter sixteen year she has not fourteen year

(939) You can borrow the book from the library.	می‌توانی کتاب را از کتابخانه قرض بگیری.	mitavaani ketaab raa az ketaabkhaane qarz begiri you can / book / D.O. / from / library / you can borrow
(940) You can buy a ticket at the counter.	می‌توانی از باجه، یک بلیت بخری.	mitavaani az baaje yek belit bekhari you can / from / booth / a / ticket / you can buy
(941) You can call me anytime.	هر وقت بخواهی، می‌توانی با من تماس بگیری.	har vaqt bekhaahi mitavaani baa man tamaas begiri any / time / you would want / you can / with / I / you can call
(942) You can catch me in the office until 5pm.	شما می‌توانید تا ساعت پنج بعد از ظهر، من را در دفترم پیدا کنید.	shomaa mitavaanid taa saa'at_e panj_e ba'd az zohr man raa dar daftaram peydaa konid you / you can / until / hour / five / after / noon / me / D.O. / at / my office / you would find
(943) You can cross the street there at the traffic light.	می‌توانی از آن چراغ راهنمایی، از خیابان عبور کنی.	mitavaani az aan cheraaq_e raahnamaayi az khiyaabaan 'obur koni you can / from / that / traffic light / from / street / you can cross
(944) You can definitely cook better than me.	تو مطمئناً می‌توانی بهتر از من آشپزی کنی.	to motma'ennan mitavaani behtar az man aashpazi koni you / surely / you can / better / from / I / you can cook
(945) You can delete the file. I don't need it anymore.	می‌توانی فایل را حذف کنی. دیگر آن را لازم ندارم.	mitavaani faayl raa hazf koni digar aan raa laazem nadaaram you can / file / D.O. / you can delete / anymore / that / D.O. / need / I don't have
(946) You can get a newspaper at the kiosk on the corner.	می‌توانید از دکه‌ی آن گوشه‌ی خیابان، روزنامه بگیرید.	mitavaanid az dakke_ye aan gushe_ye khiyaabaan ruznaame begirid you can / from / kiosk / that / corner / street / newspaper / you can get

(947) You can hardly recognize anything in the photo. It's so blurry.	به سختی می‌توان چیزی را در این عکس تشخیص داد. خیلی تار است. be sakhti mitavaan chizi raa dar in 'aks tashkhis daad. kheyli taar ast. hardly it can something D.O. in this picture it can recognize very blurry it is
(948) You can open the file by clicking here.	می‌توانید با کلیک کردن در اینجا، فایل را باز کنید. mitavaanid baa kelik kardan dar injaa, faayl raa baaz konid. you can with clicking at here file D.O. you can open
(949) You can pay by credit card or cash.	می‌توانید نقدی و یا با کارت اعتباری پرداخت کنید. mitavaanid naqdi va yaa baa kaart_e e'tebaari pardaakht konid. you can cash and or with card credit you can pay
(950) You can't eat the apple anymore. It is rotten.	دیگر نمی‌توانید سیب را بخورید. فاسد شده است. digar nemitavaanid sib raa bokhorid. faased shode ast. anymore you can't apple D.O. you can eat rotten it has become
(951) You can't read the sign from this distance.	نمی‌توانی علامت را از این فاصله بخوانی. nemitavaani 'alaamat raa az in faasele bekhaani. you can't sign D.O. from this distance you can read
(952) You don't have to be embarrassed. That happens to lots of guys.	لازم نیست خجالت بکشی. این موضوع برای خیلی‌ها اتفاق می‌افتد. laazem nist khejaalat bekeshi. in mozu' baraaye kheylihaa ettefaaq mioftad. need it is not you would be embarrassed this topic for many it happens
(953) You don't need an umbrella because of a few raindrops.	به خاطر چند قطره باران، به چتر نیاز نداری. be khaater_e chand qatre baaraan, be chatr niyaaz nadaari. because of several drop rain to umbrella need you don't have
(954) You don't need to be scared. The dog won't hurt you.	لازم نیست بترسی. این سگ به تو آسیبی نمی‌رساند. laazem nist betarsi. in sag be to aasibi nemiresaanad. need it is not you would be scared this dog to you it won't hurt

(955) You don't need to worry about your future. Just work hard and everything will work out.	نیازی نیست نگران آینده‌ی خود باشید. فقط سخت کار کنید و همه چیز درست خواهد شد.	niyaazi nist negaraan_e aayaande_ye khod baashid. faqat saakht kaar konid va hame chiz dorost khaahad shod.
(956) You get a ten percent discount.	ده درصد تخفیف می‌گیرید.	dah darsad takhfif migirid
(957) You have given me too much change.	بیش از حد پول خرد به من داده‌اید.	bish az hadd pul_e khord be man daade'id
(958) You have good qualifications for this job.	شما برای این شغل، واجد شرایط خوبی هستید.	shomaa baraaye in shoql, vaajed_e sharaayet_e khubi hastid
(959) You have misunderstood me.	منظور من را اشتباه متوجه شده‌ای.	manzur_e man raa eshtebaah motevajjeh shodeiy
(960) You have no reason to complain.	شما دلیلی برای شکایت ندارید.	shomaa dalili baraaye shekaayat nadaarid
(961) You have to click the link in order to read the article.	برای خواندن مقاله، باید روی این لینک کلیک کنید.	baraaye khaandan_e maqaale, baayad ru_ye in link kelik konid
(962) You have to do it like this, not like that.	شما باید آن کار را اینطور انجام بدهید، نه آنطور.	shomaa baayad aan kaar raa intowr anjaam bedahid, na aantowr
(963) You have to fasten your seat belt during landing.	شما باید در هنگام فرود، کمربند خود را ببندید.	shomaa baayad dar hengaam_e forud, kamarband_e khod raa bebandid

1000 Sentences

(964) You have to pay more attention to your health and not just work all the time.

شما باید توجه بیشتری به سلامتی خود داشته باشید، نه اینکه فقط کار کنید.
shomaa baayad tavajjoh_e bishtari be salaamati_ye khod daashte baashid, na inke faqat kaar konid.
you must attention more to health self you should have, not just you would work

(965) You have to show your passport at the border.

شما باید گذرنامه‌ی خود را در مرز نشان دهید.
shomaa baayad gozarnaame_ye khod raa dar marz neshaan dahid.
you must passport self D.O. at border you must show

(966) You have unfortunately not answered my question.

متاسفانه شما به سؤال من پاسخ ندادید.
moteassefaane shomaa be soaal_e man paasokh nadaadid.
unfortunately you to my question you didn't answer

(967) You immediately feel much better after a warm bath.

بلافاصله بعد از حمام گرم، احساس بهتری می‌کنید.
belaafaasele ba'd az hammaam_e garm, ehsaas_e behtari mikonid.
immediately after bath warm feeling better you do

(968) You look great! Who is your hairdresser?

عالی شده‌ای! آرایشگرت چه کسی است؟
'aali shodeiy! aaraayeshgarat che kasi ast?
great you have become your hairdresser what person s/he it is

(969) You lost your umbrella? You should go ask lost-and-found.

چترت را گم کرده‌ای؟ بهتر است بروی و از
chatrat raa gom kardeiy? behtar ast beravi va az
your umbrella D.O. you have lost it is better you should go and from

قسمت اشیاء پیدا شده، سؤال کنی.
qesmat_e ashyaa_ye peydaa shode, soaal koni.
section things found you may ask

(970) You may not park here, otherwise you'll get a ticket.

نمی‌توانید اینجا پارک کنید، در غیر این صورت
nemitavaanid injaa paark konid, dar qeyr_e in surat
you can't here you can park otherwise

جریمه می‌شوید.
jarime mishavid.
you are fined

(971) You must absolutely watch the movie. It's fantastic.

باید حتماً فیلم را تماشا کنی. فوق‌العاده است.
baayad hatman film raa tamaashaa koni. foqolaadde ast.
must absolutely movie D.O. you should watch amazing it is

(972) You must be thirsty. What would you like to drink?

شما باید تشنه باشید. نوشیدنی چه میل دارید؟
shomaa baayad teshne baashid. nushidani che meyl daarid?
you must thirsty you should be drink what you desire

(973)	شما باید تصادف را به شرکت بیمه گزارش دهید. shomaa baayad tasaadof raa be sherkat_e bime gozaaresh dahid you must accident D.O. to company insurance you should report	You must report the accident to the insurance company.
(974)	کفش خوب لازم دارید. مسیر سنگلاخ است. kafsh_e khub laazem daarid masir sanglaakh ast shoe good need you have path rocky it is	You need good shoes. The path is rocky.
(975)	شما اینجا حتی در تابستان هم به لباس گرم نیاز دارید. shomaa injaa hattaa dar taabestaan ham be lebaas_e garm niyaaz daarid you here even in summer also to clothes warm need you have	You need warm clothes here even in the summer.
(976)	شما با چشمان خود می‌بینید و با بینی خود بو می‌کشید. shomaa baa cheshmaan_e khod mibinid va baa bini_ye khod bu mikeshid you with eyes self you see and with nose self you smell	You see with your eyes and smell with your nose.
(977)	شما باید زخم را با الکل تمیز کنید. shomaa baayad zakhm raa baa alkol tamiz konid you must wound D.O. with alcohol you should clean	You should clean the wound with alcohol.
(978)	برای رسیدن به بهترین نتیجه، باید دستورالعمل‌ها را قدم به قدم دنبال کنید. baraaye residan be behtarin natije baayad dasturol'amalhaa raa qadam be qadam donbaal konid for reaching to best results must instructions D.O. step to step you should follow	You should follow the instructions step by step for the best results.
(979)	هرگز نباید تسلیم شوید. همیشه امیدی هست. hargez nabaayad taslim shavid hamishe omidi hast never must not you should surrender always hope it is	You should never give up. There is always hope.
(980)	نباید به والدین یا دوستان خود دروغ بگویید. nabaayad be vaaledeyn yaa dustaan_e khod doruq beguiyd must not to parents or friends self lie you should tell	You shouldn't lie to your parents or friends.
(981)	نباید بینی خود را در جای عمومی بگیرید. nabaayad bini_ye khod raa dar jaa_ye 'omumi begirid must not nose self D.O. in place public you should grab	You shouldn't pick your nose in public.

You turn on the machine by simply pressing a button.	(982) فقط کافیست با فشار دادن یک دکمه، دستگاه را روشن کنید. *faqat kaafist baa feshaar daadan_e yek dokme, dastgaah raa roshan konid* only it's enough with pressing a button device D.O. turn on
You used up all the hot water again.	(983) دوباره تمام آب گرم را مصرف کردی. *dobaare tamaam_e aab_e garm raa masraf kardi* again all warm water D.O. you used
You want to decorate your apartment? I'll help you. We can do it together.	(984) می‌خواهی آپارتمان خود را تزیین کنی؟ به تو کمک می‌کنم. می‌توانیم با هم این کار را انجام دهیم. *mikhaahi aapaartemaan_e khod raa taziyn koni? be to komak mikonam. mitavaanim baa ham in kaar raa anjaam dahim.* you want apartment self D.O. you would decorate to you I help we can this together activity D.O. we can do
You want to have a picnic? I think that's a great idea.	(985) می‌خواهی پیک‌نیک بروی؟ به نظرم فکر خوبیست. *mikhaahi piknik beravi? be nazaram fekr khubist* you want picnic you would go in my opinion thought it is good
You were lucky that you didn't hurt yourself.	(986) شانس آوردید که به خودتان صدمه نزدید. *shaans aavardid ke be khodetaan sadame nazadid* chance you brought that to yourself you didn't hurt
You will get a replacement from our company for the broken device.	(987) شما بجای دستگاه خراب، یک دستگاه جایگزین از شرکت ما دریافت خواهید کرد. *shomaa bejaa_ye dastgaah_e kharaab, yek dastgaah_e jaaygozin az sherkat_e maa daryaaft khaahid kard.* you instead device broken a device replacement from our company you will receive
You will have to pay five Euro for this medicine.	(988) برای این دارو باید پنج یورو بپردازید. *baraaye in daaru baayad panj yuro bepardaazid* for this drug must five Euro you must pay

1000 Sentences

(989) You will receive an official invitation from us.

شما یک دعوت‌نامه‌ی رسمی، از ما
shomaa yek da'vatnaame_ye rasmi az maa
you an invitation official from we

دریافت خواهید کرد.
daryaaft khaahid kard
you will receive

(990) You will receive your pay twice per month.

شما دو بار در ماه دستمزد خواهید گرفت.
shomaa do baar dar maah dastmozd khaahid gereft
you twice at month salary you will receive

(991) You'll receive the final decision in about a week.

تصمیم نهایی را تقریباً تا یک هفته‌ی دیگر
tasmim_e nahaayi raa taqriban taa yek hafte_ye digar
decision final D.O. almost until a week another

دریافت خواهید کرد.
daryaaft khaahid kard
you will receive

(992) Young people like to read this website.

جوانان دوست دارند این وب‌سایت را بخوانند.
javaanaan dust daarand in vebsaayt raa bekhaanand
youngsters they like this website D.O. they would read

(993) Your apartment is very cozy. I like the furniture very much.

آپارتمان شما خیلی دنج است. این مبلمان را
aapaartemaan_e shomaa kheyli denj ast in moblemaan raa
your apartment very cozy it is this furniture D.O.

خیلی دوست دارم.
kheyli dust daaram
very I like

(994) Your breath stinks. Please brush your teeth.

دهان شما خیلی بو می‌دهد. لطفاً دندان‌های خود
dahaan_e shomaa kheyli bu midahad lotfan dandaanhaa_ye khod
your mouth very smell it gives please teeth self

را مسواک بزنید.
raa mesvaak bezanid
D.O. brush

(995) Your opinion is very important to me.

نظر شما برای من بسیار مهم است.
nazar_e shomaa baraaye man besyaar mohemm ast
your opinion for I very important it is

(996) شلوارت سوراخ است. - می‌دانم، واقعاً کهنه است.
Your pants have a hole. - I know, they are really old.

shalvaarat suraakh ast midaanam vaaqe'an kohne ast
your pants hole it is I know really old it is

(997) گوشیتان زنگ می‌خورد. نمی‌خواهید جواب بدهید؟
Your phone is ringing. Are you going to answer it?

gushiyetaan zang mikhorad nemikhaahid javaab bedahid
your phone it rings you don't want you would answer

(998) معلمت نصیحت خیلی خوبی به تو کرد.
Your teacher gave you great advice.

mo'allemat nasihat_e kheyli khubi be to kard
your teacher advice very good to you s/he gave

(999) درست می‌گویی. من اشتباه می‌کنم.
You're right. I'm wrong.

dorost miguiy man eshtebaah mikonam
right you say I I make mistake

(1000) تو تنها شخصی هستی که به او اعتماد دارم.
You're the only person that I trust.

to tanhaa shakhsi hasti ke be u e'temaad daaram
you only person you are that to s/he trust I have

www.ingramcontent.com/pod-product-compliance
Lightning Source LLC
Chambersburg PA
CBHW080557090426
42735CB00016B/3269